D1283860

"It is my hope that this book will insert order and understanding into the wide array of ceramic art and artists working throughout Kentucky"

by
joe
molinaro

a pottery tour of
KENTUCKY

published by:

Crystal Communications
2891 Richmond Rd. Suite 103
Lexington, Kentucky 40509
859-266-4888
crystallex@aol.com

acknowledgements & credits

First printing August 2000

Graphic design by Paula Gron.

Copy editing by Christine Clough.

ACKNOWLEDGMENTS AND CREDITS

I wish to first thank all of the ceramic artists included in this book on Kentucky studio ceramists without whose support it would have never become a reality. I would like to acknowledge the support I received in locating the artists for the book from the Kentucky Art and Craft Foundation, the Kentucky Guild of Artists and Craftsmen and The Kentucky Craft Marketing Program. I would also like to extend my appreciation to John Roberston of the Louisville Stoneware Company, Bill Shuck of Louisville Firebrick Works, Eastern Kentucky University as well as my colleague, Tim Glotzbach, for his advice and continual support. In addition, I wish to thank my wife, Mary for her sympathetic endurance and support for this project. And lastly, to all the folks at Crystal Communications, and especially to Ed Puterbaugh for his unending patience in guiding me through the process of bringing the book to completion.

Library of Congress Catalog Card Number: 00-105218
ISBN #0-945738-75-7

Published in cooperation with *Arts Across Kentucky* magazine, a nonprofit project to promote Kentucky artisans.

**For subscription information call 859-266-4888.
Thank you for supporting Kentucky artists.**

KENTUCKY REGIONAL MAP	4
INTRODUCTION	4
BACKGROUND	6
RIVER REGION	8
RIVER ARTISTS	10
HIGHLANDS REGION	50
HIGHLANDS ARTISTS	52
CUMBERLAND REGION	70
CUMBERLAND ARTISTS	72
WESTERN LAKES REGION	80
WESTERN LAKES ARTISTS	82
BLUEGRASS REGION	100
BLUEGRASS ARTISTS	102
ABOUT THE AUTHOR	140
GLOSSARY	141
INDEX	142
GALLERY GUIDE	144

I am pleased to present this pottery guide on contemporary Kentucky studio ceramic artists and their work as a way to help identify and locate the variety of clay objects produced across the state. The guide is meant to serve the user by providing examples of artwork, contact information, gallery resources, and maps, and I hope it offers better exposure for the artists as well as more access for the consumer in contacting the artists and their work.

introduction

While a guide such as this will certainly aid in identifying those artists who presently work in clay, it is the presentation of artists by region that ultimately makes this book a practical and useful guide for studio potters and clay sculptors. Whether one is traveling from Cincinnati to Knoxville, from Nashville to Louisville, from Memphis to Chicago, or simply planning a drive through a particular part of the state, the presentation by region allows for an easy fit with one's touring schedule. Easy-to-follow color-coding helps to identify the various regions and the artists from a particular area, with individuals arranged alphabetically within each section and further identified by county. The guide features full-color examples of the artists' work, pertinent studio and showroom information, a listing of galleries and/or shops within the state that showcase ceramics, as well as photos of the artists and copies of the signatures/stamps they use to sign their pieces.

Beginning in the northernmost River Region of either Louisville or Covington, *A Pottery Tour of Kentucky* takes you southeastward into the Highlands mountain region of eastern Kentucky toward Morehead and/or Berea. Continuing westward through the Cumberland Region and cave country of Somerset and Bowling Green, the book moves onward into the Western Lakes toward Murray and Paducah. The last

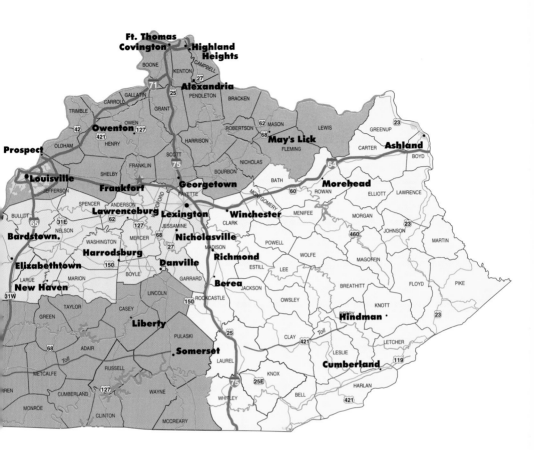

area of the state, the Bluegrass Region, brings you back around in a sort of spiral movement toward Lexington. Any section can be accessed either separately or as part of a larger area, with all of the regions consistent in presentation. Local and state maps as well as an appendix help complete the information available for use within this guide, with a full listing of galleries and a glossary of terms to help with any technical or stylistic reference.

It is my hope that *A Pottery Tour of Kentucky* will insert order and understanding into the wide array of ceramic art and artists working throughout the state.

RIVER REGION

HIGHLANDS REGION

CUMBERLAND REGION

WESTERN LAKES REGION

BLUEGRASS REGION

Kentucky prides itself on its "craft" tradition, but the production of ceramics by Kentucky studio artists often transcends notions of tradition and regionalism. Here, in a land rich in natural resources (clay deposits) and home to some of the best folk artists in the country, a ceramic spectrum continues to unfold daily. While the influences of traditional craft values are respected and preserved, many ceramists across the Bluegrass are discovering new ways to expand and to express themselves and their personal visions in clay. Artists who have migrated to Kentucky bring with them a different approach to an old medium while seeking to remain connected to the rich heritage that surrounds them. Meanwhile, many ceramists who are products of the Bluegrass continue to find new ways to bring tradition to the fore-

background

front of work that remains vital, even as we enter a new millennium. This blending of traditional craft values with a deep appreciation and understanding of contemporary art helps to create some of the finest ceramics in the Bluegrass.

The Drying Room,
Louisville Fire Brick Works –
1901-1920

Because of the region's proximity to coalfields and clay deposits, as well as the desire of locals to produce wares that reflected English and German traditions, pottery businesses began as early as the 1820s in the Louisville area. In the early 1880s, there were a number of potters working in the region, and they often moved freely from one pottery location to another. However, it was not until the late 19th century that the first pottery became established enough to become a successful business in Louisville.

A studio ceramics facility that has thrived in Kentucky over the years is the Louisville Stoneware Company. The company was founded in 1878 by John Bauer and was called the J.B. Pottery of Louisville, Kentucky. In 1905, the business was sold to Sylvester O. Snyder, who changed the name to the Louisville Pottery Company. In 1938, John B. Taylor bought it, and in 1970, he sold it to John Robertson, who changed the name to the current Louisville Stoneware Company. In 1997, the company was sold to the present owner, Christina Lee Brown (of the Brown-Forman family), and stoneware pottery continues to be made there as it was in the 1800s when John Bauer owned it.

In addition, the Hadley Pottery, also located in Louisville, continues to produce wares for the public as it has since its inception in the early 1940s by Mary Alice Hadley. M.A. Hadley began painting pottery for the Louisville Pottery Company before venturing out to establish her own pottery business in Louisville. Like other early ceramic studio businesses in the state, the Hadley Pottery was committed from the beginning to craft production on a small scale to provide objects for everyday use.

The Bybee Pottery, in the eastern region of the state in Bybee, remains the oldest working pottery west of the Alleghenies. Dating back to 1809 (with sales showing it as a thriving business by 1845), the Bybee Pottery has been producing wares for the public for well over 150 years. Bybee has been an integral part of the studio ceramics scene throughout the state and, with the present owner, Walter Cornelison, it is now in its fifth generation as a family-owned and -operated pottery business. Items are still wheel-thrown and hand-glazed, with a distinct look that marks each piece as a Bybee original.

Another lesser-known (although somewhat larger) pottery on the opposite side of the state was the Bell City Pottery, located just outside of Murray for over 80 years. This pottery once produced a line of ware that was all wheel-thrown. It changed over to more slip-cast processes before cutting back on production due to a serious fire in the mid-1990s. The owners plan to reopen it once again in the near future as a fully functioning pottery. Like the Bybee Pottery, this shop continues to be owned and operated as a family business as it has since the early days when James D. Nance ran it.

Those working in clay across the state have also enjoyed the support of several clay-related businesses. The Kentucky-Tennessee Clay Company in Mayfield produces some of the world's finest ball clays and has been a key ceramics-related industry in the state for years. Also, the Louisville Firebrick Works, which began operation as the Grahn Mines back in 1880 and later became the Louisville Firebrick Works in 1889, produces a line of materials such as bricks, mortars, casting materials, and clays. With offices in Louisville and plant operations in the eastern part of the state near Morehead, the Louisville Firebrick Works remains a vital link to the technology and materials side of kiln building for many studio ceramists working in Kentucky today.

Likewise, Ceramics Studio Supply, also in Louisville, sells a wide array of tools, equipment, and raw materials to studio potters and schools located across Kentucky. Started in 1981 as Ohio Ceramic Supply, which catered primarily to the ceramics hobby industry, the company changed ownership in 1997. It later renamed itself Ceramics Studio Supply and refocused its efforts on serving the needs of individual studio artists/potters and schools. In addition to its material and equipment offerings, CSS supports workshops, publishes a newsletter, and promotes ceramics by contributing to a number of pottery-related efforts in several communities.

Last, I would be amiss to not mention some of the important places where ceramics studies are carried out. The roots of these locations are best seen in the ceramics programs at the University of Louisville (directed by Tom Marsh from 1970 to 1991) and at the University of Kentucky (which boasts the likes of David Middlebrook, who taught ceramics in the early 1970s, and John Tuska, who taught from 1963 to 1993). Here the ceramic arts have been nurtured and promoted on local, national, and international levels, and as a result, all continue to serve those seeking to develop their careers as ceramists. Other academic institutions, such as Morehead State University, Eastern Kentucky University, Western Kentucky University, and Murray State University, also provide strong ceramics programs and facilities that continue to be important training grounds for young ceramists. It is not surprising, therefore, to see the high quality of ceramic work produced across the state by today's studio ceramists, who continue to add yet another layer to the ceramics traditions of Kentucky.

Joe Molinaro
Professor of Art, Eastern Kentucky University
June 2000

Coal-Fired Kilns,
Louisville Fire Brick Works – 1890

Home to the largest urban center in Kentucky, the northern part of the state is an interesting blend of river culture and rural and urban life. With the towns of Covington, Ft. Mitchell, and Newport (across the river from Cincinnati) to the north and Louisville on its western edge, an eclectic sense of the people and culture shines through. Simultaneously sparse and dense in population, the River Region stretches across busy city life and lush rural spaces. In addition to the blend of people and space, the political fortunes of the state are often defined in Frankfort, the state's capital, located on its southern border.

Along with the urban scene in Louisville comes the enjoyment of prestigious galleries and museums such as the J.B. Speed Museum, the Kentucky Center for the Arts, the Kentucky Art and Craft

river region

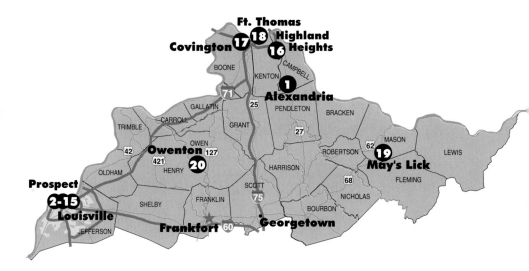

Foundation, the Louisville Visual Arts Association, and a variety of smaller art and craft venues. The state university system offers ceramics training through the University of Louisville and Northern Kentucky University in Highland Heights, with additional course work in ceramics offered at Bellarmine College. Other community-based art centers and/or training facilities are also available.

Because of the region's relative size and population, it is no surprise that a large portion of the ceramists in this book reside here (with the areas of Louisville and northern Kentucky having most of these). One can easily find a wide range of quality studio production in the River Region, with work ranging from the most traditional to the most contemporary, both in pottery and clay sculpture. Artists have been drawn to this region for decades because of its proximity to the larger cities and subsequent art markets. With the easy access to museums, galleries, and craft fairs, the River Region is a prime location for many of Kentucky's ceramic artists.

STUDIO NAME
Watson Studios Pottery
STUDIO ADDRESS
3404 Upper Tug Fork
Alexandria, KY   41001
(859) 635-5599
watsonclay@juno.com

1

larry watson

Larry Watson completed a bachelor of science degree from Eastern Kentucky University and took his first pottery class in 1981 through an adult education course. While working as a commercial printer, he continued his ceramics training on his own through evening clay classes at a local university. He sells his pottery in various galleries and shops throughout the region as well as through commissions and his own studio. He is an active member in the Kentucky Guild of Artists and Craftsmen and occasionally teaches part time at Northern Kentucky University. In 1989, he purchased a home in rural Kentucky about 20 minutes from Cincinnati, where he owns and operates Watson Studio Pottery.

Watson's work is primarily functional porcelain pottery that aspires to be elegant and unique with a whimsical flair. His line of pottery, which includes casseroles, plates, pitchers, goblets, covered jars, and more, addresses an idea that it is possible for functional forms to go beyond their obvious utility, adding beauty and art to everyday living. The surfaces of his pieces are vibrant in color with traces of clay decoration sitting quietly beneath their skins. Handles dance on and around the form and come together in a style that brings fresh personality into the home in the shape of everyday functional ware.

about the artist

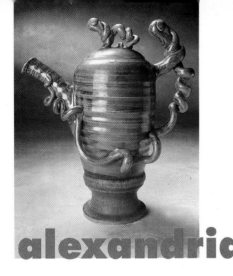

alexandria

STUDIO HOURS	BY APPOINTMENT
SHOWROOM	NO
HOURS	N/A
WORK IS SOLD	RETAIL/WHOLESALE

selected kentucky galleries

Completely Kentucky, Frankfort

Kentucky Art and Craft Foundation, Louisville

Harrodsburg Pottery & Crafts, Harrodsburg

Various State Park Gift Shops

DIRECTIONS

Call for directions.

STUDIO NAME
Yerger Andre' Pottery
STUDIO ADDRESS
133 N. Birchwood Ave.
Lousiville, KY   40206
(502) 894-0953
mausgrasman@msn.com

yerger andré

PHOTOGRAPH BY JAMES MOSES

Yerger André earned a bachelor's degree in philosophy from the University of Mississippi in 1987 and took graduate classes in ceramics until 1990. He received additional training at the Penland School of Crafts in North Carolina during the summers of 1987 and 1988. He served as an apprentice for two years at Brandon Stoneware Pottery in Brandon, Mississippi, and managed Natchez Trace Pottery for three years (1990-93). From 1993 to 1995, he served as a Peace Corps volunteer in Papua, New Guinea, training managers and artisans to operate a traditional crafts cooperative in a remote rainforest village. He conducted various workshops and taught classes at institutions like Bellarmine College in Louisville and John C. Campbell Folk School in Brasstown, North Carolina, and at the Mississippi Craftsmen's Guild in Ridgeland, Mississippi. In 1996 he settled in Louisville and opened Yerger André Pottery, which he still operates today. André has won several awards for his ceramics including a purchase award for a sagger-fired vessel at the Jackson Municipal Art Gallery and an honorable mention for raku pottery at the Crosstie Art Festival in Cleveland, Mississippi.

André produces a full line of functional ware (bowls, platters, plates, cups) that utilizes traditional stoneware glazes fired to cone 10 in both reduction and oxidation atmospheres. Classical forms are his trademark, with strong attention to utility carefully considered. André also produces a wide range of decorative porcelain bottles and vases with crystalline glazes on the surface. These forms are elegant and graceful, with skins that range from a high gloss with large crystals to ones that appear matte, or marblelike. His interest in the surface and how it works to highlight and showcase form is apparent in the pieces he produces.

about the artist

louisville

STUDIO HOURS	BY APPOINTMENT
SHOWROOM	YES
HOURS	10 AM-5 PM
WORK IS SOLD	RETAIL/WHOLESALE

selected kentucky galleries

Kentucky Art and Craft Foundation, Louisville

DIRECTIONS
One-half block north off Frankfort Ave. between Frankfort and Brownsboro in Crescent Hill.

3

STUDIO NAME
One Sky Pottery
STUDIO ADDRESS
237 Fairfax Avenue
Louisville, KY 40207
(502) 893-3836
hlaustin@gateway.net

lisa austin

Lisa Austin, a native of Louisville, received a bachelor's degree in English and, in 1975, a master's degree in humanities from the University of Louisville. Between 1981 and 1989, she completed 30 hours in ceramics as a postgraduate student at the University of Louisville, where she studied with Tom Marsh. She attended workshops at the University of Wisconsin in 1982 and the Idyllwild School of Music and Art in California in 1989, where she studied with renowned Acoma Pueblo potter Lucy Lewis.

Austin has participated in several juried exhibitions in the region and has received several awards, including the Early Times Scholarship and a professional development grant from the Kentucky Arts Council. Her work is in the collections of the University of Evansville and the University of Kentucky, as well as in other private collections in the state. Austin has been reviewed in major ceramics publications and remains active with the Kentucky Guild of Artists and Craftsmen and the Kentucky Art and Craft Foundation. She operates One Sky Pottery in Louisville, which she started in 1983.

Austin's work is wheel-thrown porcelain vessels fired first in an electric kiln and then again in a primitive pit. She spent a year living and working as a high-school teacher on the Canoncito Navajo Reservation in New Mexico, where she learned about Indian pottery-making traditions. Upon returning to Louisville, she developed a style of pottery making that reflected Indian influences. Her elegant vessels, made of white clay, have soft marks of smoke embellishing their surfaces. Small additions of wire and stone sometimes adorn a piece, creating shiny, jewel-like elements that help identify the forms as contemporary pieces with ancient traditions.

about the artist

louisville

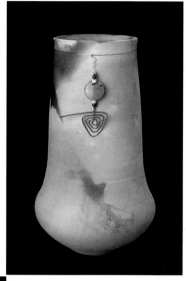

STUDIO HOURS	BY APPOINTMENT
SHOWROOM	NO
HOURS	N/A
WORK IS SOLD	RETAIL/WHOLESALE

selected kentucky galleries

Kentucky Art and Craft Foundation, Louisville

Kentucky Center for the Arts, Louisville

DIRECTIONS
Call for directions.

STUDIO NAME
Fong Choo, Potter
STUDIO ADDRESS
P.O. Box 1296
Louisville, KY   40201
(502) 635-6963
fongc@bellarmine.edu

fong choo

Fong Choo, a native of the Republic of Singapore, received a bachelor's degree in business from Warren Wilson College, Swannanoa, North Carolina, in 1988. He went on to complete a master's degree from the University of Louisville in 1993. In addition to maintaining a studio in Louisville since 1985, Choo has been an adjunct faculty member at Bellarmine College in Louisville since 1990. He regularly conducts workshops on his forming techniques and offers lectures on his ceramic work in Kentucky and the surrounding area. He has been in countless shows during this time and has received more than 15 awards for his ceramic works. In addition, he is represented in numerous galleries throughout the Midwest.

Inspired by his Chinese heritage, Choo produces miniature teapots as his signature pieces. These miniatures have a long-standing tradition in the great Yixing (Yi-Sing) style of pottery. Choo, however, reinterprets the tradition by incorporating jewel-tone glazes rich in surface variations. While the forms he produces are small in scale, they carry a large presence through the detail of form and surface and the highly sophisticated manner in which they come together.

Choo airbrushes his glazes onto each piece to create an interesting overlap effect. The work is most often fired in gas kilns to a high temperature, giving it the authentic look of larger, high-fired functional ware. Working in a tedious fashion, much like a jeweler, he is forced to pay particular attention to each aspect of the process, working meticulously to combine forms and the detailed glazing techniques he uses. This is vital to ensure success working on such a small scale.

about the artist

louisville

STUDIO HOURS	BY APPOINTMENT
SHOWROOM	YES
HOURS	BY APPOINTMENT
WORK IS SOLD	RETAIL/WHOLESALE

selected kentucky galleries

Kentucky Art and Craft Foundation, Louisville

Images Friedman Gallery, Louisvlle

DIRECTIONS
From Louisville, take I-65 south to the
Watterson Expressway (I-264 E) to the
Newburg Road Exit 15. Turn left on
Newburg Road heading North. Look for
Bellarmine College signs and then the Art
Department.

STUDIO NAME
Coakes Pottery
STUDIO ADDRESS
Hite Art Institute
University of Louisville
Louisville, KY 40201
(502) 375-1628 / home
(502) 852-6796 / studio
mdcoak01@athena.louisville.edu

michelle coakes

Michelle Coakes first studied ceramics at Northern Illinois University, where she completed a bachelor of fine arts degree in 1982, a master of arts degree in 1985, and a master of fine arts degree in 1987. She went on to further her ceramics education as a special student in art at Wichita State University, where she studied with Chris Staley. She worked as an apprentice at Eckel's Pot Shop in Bayfield, Wisconsin, from 1982 to 1983 and served as an artist-in-residence at the Florida Gulf Coast Art Center in Belleair, Florida, from 1989 to 1991. She taught full time at Western Kentucky University from 1991 to 1995 and at Waubonsee Community College from 1995 to 1997. She is currently head of the ceramics program at the University of Louisville. Coakes's work has been exhibited widely throughout the United States, and she has received numerous awards for her artwork. She is regularly asked to conduct workshops, give lectures, and serve on panels at various ceramics-related events. She is also the author of the ceramics book titled *Creative Pottery* (Gloucester, Massachusetts: Rockport Publishers, 1998).

Coakes is best known for her functional and quasi-functional vessels in stoneware, most of which are finished in a wood-fired (anagama) kiln. Almost all of her work is wheel-thrown and manipulated. Forms reminiscent of antique oil and watering cans are the inspiration for her most recent works in clay. The rich, variable, wood-fired surfaces add greatly to the illusion and references she sets up between old and new. Spouts, which take on a gestural quality, only add to the sculptural presence in the work. References to tradition and utility are constants in all of her clay work.

Coakes also produces a wide range of more traditional utilitarian pots that are high-fired in gas kilns. A love for functional work is evident in these pieces. Stacking bowls, teapots, and cruet sets are but a few of the many utilitarian forms produced for everyday use. Coakes continues the search for dynamic sculptural forms in all the work she produces.

about the artist

louisville

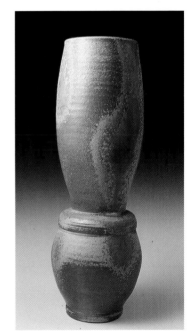

STUDIO HOURS	BY APPOINTMENT
SHOWROOM	NO
HOURS	N/A
WORK IS SOLD	RETAIL

selected kentucky galleries

Kentucky Art and Craft Foundation, Louisville

Imagés Friedman Gallery, Louisville

DIRECTIONS
I-65 exit Eastern Parkway in Louisville.
Follow signs to University of Louisville. Studio
Arts Building is diagonally across from
McDonald's on campus.

STUDIO NAME
Clay House Pots Studio
STUDIO ADDRESS
317 S. Jane St.
Louisville, KY   40206
(502) 893-0888
amye@thepoint.net

amy elswick

Amy Elswick began her ceramics career as a student at Berea College, where she worked as an apprentice in the ceramics studio from 1987 to 1991. After graduating from Berea College in 1991 with a bachelor's degree in Spanish, she continued her ceramics training at the Metro Arts Center (MAC) in Louisville. She later taught ceramics at the MAC as well as at the Beechmont Community Center, both of which were operated by the Jefferson County Metro Parks Department. Elswick worked as a studio artist for the sculpture art business 9 Pines Art in Louisville from 1995 to 1997; in 1998 she established Clay House Pots Studio, which she owns and operates today. She is a member of the Kentucky Art and Craft Foundation, the Kentucky Craft Marketing program, the Louisville Visual Art Association, and the Sheltowee Artisans. Her work is featured in numerous craft fairs in the region, including the St. James Court Fair in Louisville; the Penrod Society Art Fair in Indianapolis, Indiana; the Dayton Art Institute Oktoberfest in Dayton, Ohio; and the International Gift Fair in New York City.

Elswick produces a line of functional pottery using a variety of wheel-thrown and hand-built forming techniques. Pieces are all stoneware fired to cone 6 (2,175 Fahrenheit) in electric kilns. Elswick works hard to create forms that convey festivity and celebration to her pottery, which is meant for everyday use. She is intent on producing pottery that is utilitarian and that can be used for the daily activities of eating and drinking. Legged bowls, vases, cups, and saucers, along with items such as birdfeeders and other household forms (sinks, for example), are just some of the pottery items produced at Clay House Pots.

about the artist

louisville

PHOTOGRAPH BY WALTER J. OLIN

STUDIO HOURS	BY APPOINTMENT
SHOWROOM	NO
HOURS	N/A
WORK IS SOLD	RETAIL/WHOLESALE

selected kentucky galleries

Kentucky Art and Craft Foundation, Louisville

Completely Kentucky, Frankfort

Promenade Gallery, Berea

Artique, Lexington

DIRECTIONS
I-64 to Grinstead Drive (from the east), turn left on Grinstead and then first left on Peterson. Left on Frankfort Ave., and then left on Ewing. Turn right on Bickel to first unmarked alley on right. Second house on left. (Access to studio is on alley side behind Jane St.)

STUDIO NAME
Wayne Ferguson Pottery
STUDIO ADDRESS
203 N. Pope
Louisville, KY   40206
(502) 394-8187

wayne ferguson

Wayne Ferguson attended Edgecliff College in Cincinnati, Ohio, and the University of Kentucky. He has conducted a variety of workshops in the region including ones at the Penland School of Crafts in North Carolina and at Key West Community College in Florida. He has exhibited his work extensively throughout the Midwest in one-person and group shows, and he is frequently asked to give presentations to various groups about his artwork.

Ferguson is the recipient of several prestigious awards including the Al Smith Fellowship from the Kentucky Arts Council and a Brown-Forman Early Times Scholarship. His work has been featured in a number of publications including the book *Kentucky Crafts: Handmade and Heartfelt* by Phyllis George (New York: Crown Publishers, 1989). His pieces can also be easily found in a number of galleries throughout the state.

Ferguson produces handmade, semifunctional vessel forms that incorporate animal and human elements. Using colorful glazed surfaces, the pieces are generally fired in raku, majolica, and other low-fired processes. Ferguson's ceramic work is known for its playfulness and humor, yet aspects of utility are often carefully contained within each piece. Contemporary icons and imagery often find their way into his work, adding elements of humor to its visual content. Rich textural surfaces along with points of color are carefully orchestrated to enhance the narrative, helping to make each piece a functional form and a ceramic sculpture.

about the artist

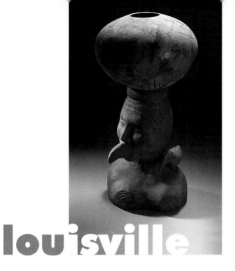

louisville

STUDIO HOURS	8 AM-5 PM
SHOWROOM	YES
HOURS	BY APPOINTMENT
WORK IS SOLD	RETAIL/WHOLESALE

selected kentucky galleries

Kentucky Art and Craft Foundation, Louisville

Capital Gallery, Frankfort

Swanson-Cralle Gallery, Louisville

DIRECTIONS
I-64 going north, go right off the Mellwood
Exit. Go to the first light ((Frankfort Ave.) and
turn right, up the hill to the first stoplight.
Turn left onto Pope St. Go about 100 feet,
studio on the right.

8

STUDIO NAME
Sarah Frederick Studio Pottery
STUDIO ADDRESS
2735 Field Ave.
Louisville, KY   40206
(502) 897-1298

sarah frederick

Sarah Frederick received a bachelor's degree from Mills College in Oakland, California, in 1957, where she studied with noted ceramist Antonio Prieto. In 1978, she earned a master's degree from the University of Louisville under the guidance of Tom Marsh. She also received training at the Massachusetts College of Art in Boston; Haystack Mountain School of Crafts in Deer Isle, Maine; and Murray State University in Murray. Her work has been on display at the Smithsonian Institution and at Neiman-Marcus in San Francisco and has been a part of several prestigious art collections. She has received numerous awards for her ceramics, such as the Kentucky Arts Council's Al Smith Fellowship in 1992, and was one of the featured artists in the book *Kentucky Crafts: Handmade and Heartfelt* by Phyllis George (New York: Crown Publishers, 1989). She continues to exhibit her work regularly in a variety of art exhibitions held throughout the country. She often attends and conducts workshops in ceramics and teaches as an adjunct faculty member at the University of Louisville.

From 1980 to 1995, Frederick directed the production of a line of pottery of her own design that was inspired by decorative art and organic form. She is best known for this line of low-fire work, which was marketed nationally before being retired from production in 1995. She currently spends more time in the studio producing figurative landscape sculptural pieces that are high-fired. She also produces fine porcelain functional ware that is often fired in a gas and/or wood kiln.

With a flair for design and interesting surface treatments, Frederick has managed to produce a variety of forms over the years that offer a fresh look into what might otherwise be viewed as mundane. Whether creating low- or high-fired functional forms, or sculptural pieces using a mixed-media approach, Frederick is the consummate artist who continually seeks out new ways of creating personal expression in clay.

about the artist

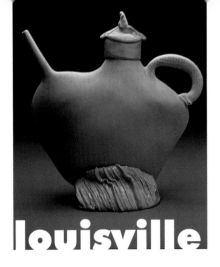

louisville

STUDIO HOURS	BY APPOINTMENT
SHOWROOM	NO
HOURS	N/A
WORK IS SOLD	RETAIL/WHOLESALE

selected kentucky galleries

Kentucky Art and Craft Foundation, Louisville

Swanson-Cralle Gallery, Louisville

DIRECTIONS
Just off Frankfort Ave. which is accessed from I-64 at the Grinstead or Cannons Lane Exits.

STUDIO NAME
Pegls Studio
STUDIO ADDRESS
340 Franck Ave.
Louisville, KY   40206
(502) 896-9530
pj@iglou.com

peggy thieneman leake

Peggy Leake received a bachelor's degree in biology from Spalding University in 1969. She began studying ceramics at the University of Louisville in 1977 and completed a master's degree in 1997. She has exhibited her work in prestigious national and international ceramics competitions such as the International Orton Cone Box Show in Baldwin City, Kansas, in 1994; the Mashiko Ceramics Competition in Mashiko, Japan, in 1996 and 1998; USA Craft Today in New Canaan, Connecticut, in 1997; and the Arrowmont School of Arts and Crafts National in 1999.

Leake has won several awards and is represented in the Orton Cone Box collection. Her work can be found at various galleries throughout the state.

Leake produces wheel-thrown miniature (egg-size) porcelain bottles and vases. Some pieces are glazed by airbrushing various layers of glaze onto the surface, while others are carved with organic motifs. Her pieces are strong, traditional volumetric forms that often take on a seedpod presence through glaze, shape, and overall size. Leake grew up on a farm, and she continues to turn toward nature for inspiration in her clay work. She said, "The organic forms reflected in my clay pieces find their origins in my past." Pieces are frequently wood-fired to create a variable surface depth, which offers a highly sophisticated appearance on the symmetrical, bold, diminutive forms. In addition, the size adds "preciousness" to each piece, which in turn creates many jewel-like effects.

about the artist

louisville

STUDIO HOURS	BY APPOINTMENT
SHOWROOM	YES
HOURS	BY APPOINTMENT
WORK IS SOLD	RETAIL/WHOLESALE

selected kentucky galleries

Images Friedman Gallery, Louisville

Kentucky Art and Craft Foundation, Louisville

DIRECTIONS
Call for directions.

10

STUDIO NAME
Ginny Marsh Studio
Pottery
STUDIO ADDRESS
1814 Lauderdale Road
Louisville, KY 40205
(502) 458-4642 or
(812) 967-3928
gmarsh@aye.net

ginny marsh

MARSH

Ginny Marsh, born in Sherman, Texas, and raised in Omaha, Nebraska, was educated in ceramics at DePauw University where she received her bachelor's degree in 1967. Afterward, she attended Ohio State University in Columbus, Ohio, and completed a master of fine arts degree in 1969. She has conducted workshops throughout the United States and Canada at such prestigious institutions as the Arrowmont School of Arts and Crafts; the Greenwich House Pottery in New York City; and the Banff Centre School of Fine Art and Calgary College of Art and Design, both in Alberta, Canada. From 1980 to 1995, she worked as an editorial advisor for the Chilton Book Company and taught at the University of Louisville from 1975 to 1995.

Marsh has written several articles for various ceramics publications such as *Ceramics: Art & Perception* (Sydney, Australia), *Pottery Making Illustrated*, and *Studio Potter Magazine*. She has exhibited her work extensively throughout the United States and abroad and is represented in a number of collections, including the Smithsonian Institution in Washington, D.C. She currently operates the Ginny Marsh Pottery Studio.

Marsh's ceramic work is primarily hand-built and wheel-thrown stoneware and porcelain vessels. She is known for her finely crafted clay pieces, which are meant either for the table or for a decorative place in the home or garden. Her concern for the utilitarian object is ever present in her ceramics. She said, "When you use a pottery cup, you can tell how the maker held it and touched it, and you sense the hands of the person who made it." Her work is usually gas- or wood-fired, with textures that speak of the material from which it came. Bold forms with selected glazed areas of color against a natural clay surface are noted features that mark her ceramic work. An accomplished potter with years of training toward perfecting her art, Marsh continues to produce pottery for exhibition and sale.

about the artist

louisville

STUDIO HOURS	BY APPOINTMENT
SHOWROOM	NO
HOURS	N/A
WORK IS SOLD	WHOLESALE

selected kentucky galleries

Images Friedman Gallery, Louisville

DIRECTIONS
Call for directions.

STUDIO NAME
Wild Heron Pottery
STUDIO ADDRESS
2510 Belknap Beach Road
Prospect, KY   40059
(502) 228-4812
fax / (502) 228-3236
mineross@earthlink.net

judy miner

Judy Miner began her ceramics training by taking classes at the University of Kentucky from 1961 to 1964. She received a bachelor's degree in 1980 and a master's degree in 1994, both from the University of Louisville. She still continues her education in ceramics by attending a variety of workshops throughout the United States. Minor exhibits her work in exhibitions within the state and is represented in galleries in Louisville and Berea. In 1993 she opened Wild Heron Pottery in Louisville, where she continues to work today.

Miner's work in ceramics is mostly functional porcelain and some stoneware such as dinnerware and serving dishes. She produces other work used in the home as well, such as tiles, sinks, and cabinet knobs. She fires most of her pieces in reduction gas-fired kilns, some of her other work in wood and salt kilns.

Miner produces pieces that function well for users and that add pleasure to their lives as well as beauty to their homes. Addressing the utilitarian concerns associated with form and surface are aspects of her work that she finds fulfilling. Because it is important to her to please the senses of sight and touch, she often seeks out interesting forms and textures for her pottery. Elegance is a main focus, and whether it be a place setting for the table or a wall of tiles for a room, her pieces present themselves well within the home.

about the artist

prospect

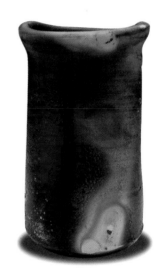

STUDIO HOURS	BY APPOINTMENT
SHOWROOM	YES
HOURS	BY APPOINTMENT
WORK IS SOLD	RETAIL/WHOLESALE

selected kentucky galleries

Kentucky Art and Craft Foundation, Louisville

Images Friedman Gallery, Louisville

Contemporary Artifacts Gallery, Berea

Swanson Cralle Gallery, Louisville

DIRECTIONS

East on U.S. 42 to Rose Island Road. Two miles to Belknap Beach Road.

STUDIO NAME
New Leaf Pottery
STUDIO ADDRESS
2510 Belknap Beach Road
Prospect, KY   40059
(502) 228-5034
fax - (502) 228-3236
mineross@earthlink.net

laura ross

about the artist

Laura Ross received her bachelor's degree in merchandising from the University of Kentucky in 1969. She went on to earn a master's degree in ceramics from the University of Louisville in 1981, where she studied with Tom Marsh. She continued her ceramics studies over the years by attending a variety of workshops and conferences across the country. After teaching in the public schools for 11 years, Ross gave up teaching to begin her career as a studio potter. She has exhibited her ceramics regularly over the past 15 years and has participated in several select national retail shows and art fairs. Ross has received several awards for her ceramics, including a Purchase Award from *Ceramics Monthly* magazine in 1999, a Niche Finalist award in 1992, and a Governor's Award through the Kentucky Department of the Arts in 1987. In addition, she received an Early Times Scholarship from the Kentucky Art and Craft Foundation in 1995.

Ross's ceramic work is mostly wheel-thrown and altered stoneware and porcelain functional ware (vases, bottles, casseroles, platters, soy jars, teapots, etc.) that are reduction gas-fired, wood-fired, and sometimes salt-glazed. Her pieces carry a strong presence of form complete with surfaces that offer abundant visual interest. Through the wood-firing process, she is able to capture the quality of wood ash and flame as they interfere and interact with the work. Her desire to create forms that are visually stimulating and useful is evident in her work. Ross said, "It is my intent to create pottery that is selected because it functions effortlessly in the dance of daily use, as well as having energy and life force that make a connection with the user."

prospect

STUDIO HOURS	9 AM - 5 PM
SHOWROOM	YES
HOURS	9 AM - 5 PM
WORK IS SOLD	RETAIL/WHOLESALE

selected kentucky galleries

Kentucky Art and Craft Foundation, Louisville

Swanson Cralle Gallery, Louisville

Images Friedman Gallery, Louisville

DIRECTIONS
East on U.S. 42 to Rose Island Road. Two
miles to Belknap Beach Road.

STUDIO NAME
Mary F. Rounsavall
STUDIO ADDRESS
7501 Covered Bridge Road
Prospect, KY   40059
(502) 228-4371
mfrouns@attglobal.net
http://www.maryrounsavall.com

mary f. rounsavall

Mary Rounsavall received a bachelor's degree from Sarah Lawrence College in Bronxville, New York, in 1966. She attended ceramics workshops at the Anderson Ranch in Colorado and at the Penland School of Crafts in North Carolina. She also worked as an apprentice for Sergei Isupov from 1994 to 1996. She has exhibited her work regularly in the Louisville area and has won several awards for her ceramics. Her work is sold through galleries and wholesale/retail shows as well as at her studio, with some work completed as part of various commissions.

Rounsavall's ceramic work is an interesting blend of utility and humor. Pieces are mostly hand formed using stoneware and porcelain clays with a wide range of surface treatments, including stains, commercial glazes, and lusters. Decorative and hand-formed ornamentation, along with slip trailing, are common elements of her pottery pieces. Her ceramic work is both functional and sculptural, with the figure being a common form utilized in both types of work.

Finding humor in her ceramic pieces is important for Rounsavall; she said, " My pieces amuse me, and the mark of a successful piece for me is if it can make me smile." Her work provides a unique and colorful look at pottery, a playful attempt to bring ceramic forms, both utilitarian and sculptural, into the home.

about the artist

prospect

PHOTOGRAPHS BY GEOFF CARR

STUDIO HOURS	BY APPOINTMENT
SHOWROOM	NO
HOURS	N/A
WORK IS SOLD	RETAIL/WHOLESALE

selected kentucky galleries

Edenside Gallery, Louisville

DIRECTIONS
Call for directions.

STUDIO NAME
Pottery Rowe
STUDIO ADDRESS
2048 Frankfort Ave.
Louisville, KY   40206
(502) 896-0877
hawk390@aol.com
http://members.aol.com/
hawk390/index.htm

melvin d. rowe

Melvin Rowe has been making and selling artwork since 1971. He received his bachelor of fine arts degree from Western Kentucky University in 1973 and completed a master's degree from the University of Louisville in 1978. He has exhibited his ceramics steadily over the past 25 years and has work in several collections, such as the White House; the Karlsberg Museum in Koblenz, Germany; and the Rev. and Mrs. Alfred Shands's collection in Louisville. He has conducted several workshops in the Louisville area and has received awards from the Kentucky Craft Marketing Program in 1992 and 1997. He served as director of the Metro Arts Center in Louisville from 1977 to 1981 and taught part time at Spalding University in Louisville from 1980 to 1986. He currently owns and operates his own production studio in Louisville called Pottery Rowe, which he began in 1981. He sells his work in wholesale and retail outlets throughout the country and is a member of the Kentucky Guild of Artists and Craftsmen and the Louisville Craftsmen Guild.

Rowe's pottery is a large mix of styles from primitive spiritual art to whimsical to decorative and functional ware. He makes stoneware pieces that are meant for daily use, such as cups, bowls, plates, pitchers, and vases, all high-fired to temperatures above 2,000 degrees Fahrenheit. He also works in mixed media combining various forms and materials together to create a wide array of objects. While he has always produced utilitarian wares, he has recently devoted more time and effort to the production of ceramic pieces that place more emphasis on his artistic vision than on utility.

about the artist

louisville

STUDIO HOURS	MONDAY-SATURDAY 10 AM - 5 PM
SHOWROOM	YES
HOURS	MONDAY-SATURDAY 10 AM - 5 PM
WORK IS SOLD	RETAIL/WHOLESALE

selected kentucky galleries

Kentucky Art and Craft Foundation, Louisville

Completely Kentucky, Frankfort

Louisville Visual Art Association, Louisville

Kentucky Gallery of Fine Art & Craft, Lexington

Bebe's Artisan Market, Paducah

DIRECTIONS
From I-64 westbound, Melwood Exit, right on Melwood Ave., one-half block to light. Right on Frankfort Ave., located 6 blocks ahead on right.

STUDIO NAME
Byron Temple Pottery
STUDIO ADDRESS
P.O. Box 7914
Louisville, KY   40257
(502) 893-2684

byron temple

Byron Temple first attended Ball State University in Muncie, Indiana; the Brooklyn Museum Art School; and the Art Institute of Chicago. From 1959 to 1961, he apprenticed with the renowned British potter Bernard Leach in St. Ives, Cornwall, England; later, he continued his work with British potter Colin Pearson. He has taught at the Philadelphia College of Art, the Pratt Institute in New York City, the Haystack Mountain School in Maine, and the Penland School of Crafts in North Carolina. He owned and operated a successful production pottery studio in Lambertville, New Jersey, from 1962 to 1989 and has since relocated to Louisville where he owns his own studio pottery.

Temple's career has been marked with a great deal of success, and he is one of the nation's leading production potters. His work is included in a variety of prestigious collections, including the Smithsonian Institution in Washington, D.C.; the Everson Museum in Syracuse, New York; the Taipei Fine Arts Museum in Taiwan; the Museum Boymans van Beuningen in Rotterdam, Netherlands; and the Kunstindustrimuseeum in Copenhagen, Denmark. He is regularly asked to conduct workshops and lectures and has had countless exhibitions of his work in group and individual shows in the United States and abroad.

Temple's ceramic work is primarily high-temperature utilitarian wares that are often fired in wood-, salt-, and saggar-fired kilns. His pieces are prime examples of how traditional pottery can extol the virtues of proportion and harmony through its elegant, yet simple approaches to functionalism. Temple said, "Pots are like children: they have to make their own path in the world, eventually." His work reflects a modern aesthetic that melds tradition and contemporary thought in beautifully defined utilitarian forms. Pieces are most often minimalist through their use of color, glaze, and form. They suggest an unconscious, almost anonymous nature while still conveying a sense of humanity and personal identity.

louisville

STUDIO HOURS	BY APPOINTMENT
SHOWROOM	NO
HOURS	NO
WORK IS SOLD	WHOLESALE

selected kentucky galleries

Vine Gallery, Louisville

DIRECTIONS
Call for directions.

STUDIO NAME
Ana England Studios
STUDIO ADDRESS
4104 B (5th Floor)
Springrove Ave.
Cincinnati, OH   45223
(513) 541-1056

Northern Kentucky
University, Art Department
Nunn Drive, CS103
Highland Heights, KY 41099
(859) 572-5425
englanda@nku.edu

ana england

Ana England, a native of Middlesboro, received her bachelor's degree from New College in Sarasota, Florida, in 1975. She went on to study art at San Francisco State University in California from 1979 to 1981. She completed a master's degree in ceramics in 1983 and a master of fine arts in sculpture in 1984, both from San Jose State University, San Jose, California. She worked as an assistant to the director at the San Jose Institute of Contemporary Art and as an assistant to renowned sculptor David Middlebrook in Los Gatos, California. She currently teaches at Northern Kentucky University, where she has been on the faculty since 1986.

England's ceramic work has been exhibited widely throughout the United States dating back to 1980. She has completed numerous commissions spanning nearly 20 years and is represented in several prestigious collections. Her works have been reviewed in art journals and newspapers across the country, with many notable awards accompanying them. She frequently gives workshops and lectures, remains active in countless professional activities, and often serves as either a juror or a panelist for conferences.

Ana England's work is primarily sculptural in nature, often utilizing a mixed-media approach to form and surface. The pieces are frequently made of multiple elements, most often freestanding, with a scale that is human size. Her most recent sculptural forms attempt to create a visual language with a synthesis between science and metaphysics. As England said about her work, "I am not attempting to make science but rather to visually ruminate on our transition from primordial soup to individuated being, and perhaps back again." England's work often appears organic while making selective references to the more scientific areas of life. Her larger-than-life ceramic sculptural forms are elegant statements that make provocative references to the much larger world in which we live. Her use of ceramic materials and techniques makes her work at once visually stimulating and intellectually challenging.

about the artist

northern kentucky

STUDIO HOURS	BY APPOINTMENT
SHOWROOM	NO
HOURS	N/A
WORK IS SOLD	RETAIL

selected kentucky galleries

Kentucky Art and Craft Foundation, Louisville

DIRECTIONS
Call for directions.

STUDIO NAME
Main Street Pottery
STUDIO ADDRESS
809 Main Street
Covington, KY   41011
(859) 491-4305
cmomsp@earthlink.net

colette oliver

Colette Oliver, a native of Cleveland, Ohio, received her bachelor's degree from Thomas Moore College in 1979. She sells primarily in wholesale and retail shows in Kentucky, Ohio, and Indiana and at a number of galleries and shops across the United States. She was co-owner of Steinkrug Pottery from 1980 to 1985, when she opened her own studio, Main Street Pottery, in Covington, which she still owns and operates today. She is a member of the Kentucky Craft Marketing Program and the Craft Guild of Greater Cincinnati.

Oliver's pottery is primarily functional ware; she has a strong belief in the importance of utilitarian pottery for everyday use. She said, "The greatest influence on my work is the belief that art should be available to everyone for use in daily life. Given my passion for clay, this belief has made me a functional potter."

Oliver's pieces are all made of earthenware clay that is carefully hand painted. Most have a floral design painted onto the surface and are oxidation-fired to above 2,000 degrees Fahrenheit. The pottery is all thrown on the wheel and is oven-, microwave-, and dishwasher-safe. Works range from mugs to cookie jars to chip-and-dip sets and other functional items. Her work is largely influenced by early American folk pottery as well as painting, primarily the loose brushwork of Robert Motherwell, John Singer Sargent, and Edouard Manet. She continues to find ways to expand upon her painted pottery and regularly looks to add more designs.

about the artist

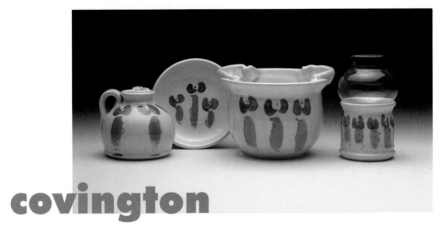

covington

STUDIO HOURS	BY APPOINTMENT
SHOWROOM	NO
HOURS	N/A
WORK IS SOLD	RETAIL/WHOLESALE

selected kentucky galleries

Cove Gallery, Northside, OH

Crooked Tree Gallery, Covington

Woodbourne Gallery, Cincinnati, Ohio

Various Kentucky State Park Gift Shops

Where In the World Gift Shop, Maysville

Land Between the Lakes, Golden Pond

DIRECTIONS

Take the Fifth St. Exit off I-75 (1st exit south of the Ohio River). On Fifth St. turn right at the second traffic light (Main St.). Go to the fifth house on right after Eighth St.

(18)

STUDIO NAME
Diane Kruer Studios
STUDIO ADDRESS
227 Rosemont Ave.
Ft. Thomas, KY   41075
(859) 781-0929
dianekruer@mail.7hills.org

diane kruer

Diane Kruer received her bachelor of fine arts degree in 1975 and a bachelor of arts degree in 1978, both from Northern Kentucky University. She then went on to complete a master of fine arts degree from the University of Cincinnati in 1981 and has continued her education by attending numerous ceramics workshops dating back to 1972. She has worked as an instructor in ceramics at the University of Cincinnati from 1980 to 1981, as an artist-in-residence for the Ohio Arts Council from 1981 to 1986, and as an art instructor at Northern Kentucky University from 1985 to 1986. She is presently an instructor of visual arts at Seven Hills School in Cincinnati, where she has been on the faculty since 1986. She has served as a visiting artist, guest lecturer, and juror for numerous arts organizations dating back to 1978. Kruer's work has been featured in more than 75 exhibitions over the past 20 years and in several art collections in the region. In addition, she has been published in major ceramics publications and has been the recipient of more than 15 awards over the past 20 years.

Kruer's ceramic works are mostly hand-built porcelain sculptural vessels that are fired to 2,400 degrees Fahrenheit and finished with lusters and paint. These forms often address the nature and significance of balance, literally and metaphorically. Pieces are often positioned on a fine point, a small foothold, where they often rise from a point of roughness at the base to a delicate opening. A balance of contrasts and contradictions is worth noting, as the pieces often allude to issues outside of the immediate clay forms. Work that is quiet in its attempt to balance a precarious equilibrium of opposing forces and spaces is the trademark of her delicate porcelain vessels.

about the artist

ft. thomas

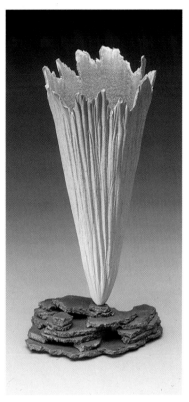

STUDIO HOURS	NOT AVAILABLE
SHOWROOM	NO
HOURS	N/A
WORK IS SOLD	RETAIL

selected kentucky galleries

Risch Gallery, Ft. Thomas

DIRECTIONS
Call for directions.

STUDIO NAME
Ann LeGris
STUDIO ADDRESS
5101 Shouse Lane
May's Lick, KY   41055
(606) 763-6785
annlegris@hotmail.com

ann leGris

Ann LeGris began making pottery in the early 1970s while still a member of the Madison Potter's Guild Co-Op in Madison, Wisconsin. She was a full-time production potter in the 1980s making functional stoneware and porcelain that she sold throughout the Midwest at various art shows, museums, and art centers. She moved to Kentucky in 1982 and has since given up functional pottery production to focus on creating white earthenware vessels that are pit-fired. She has exhibited her work in various art shows in the region and has work in several prestigious collections, including the Cleveland Museum of Art, the Canton Museum of Art, and the Kentucky Fried Chicken Corporate Collection. She has taught and conducted workshops at a variety of institutions, such as the Maysville Community College Continuing Education Program, Xavier University in Cincinnati, the Kentucky State Department of Parks, and the Mason County Arts Council.

LeGris's ceramic works are mostly wheel-thrown classical forms of white earthenware. Each piece is burnished with an applied decoration of slips, drawn images, and/or color washes. After the forms are fired in an electric kiln to approximately 1,800 degrees Fahrenheit, they are individually pit-fired to achieve the sensuous, colored surface of the clay.

Her current work displays an interest in the natural world and represents abstractions of the rural scenes that surround her. LeGris said, "Undulating native grasses, praying mantises, grazing horses, and the clear night sky all provide inspiration for the decorative aspects of my pottery." Her works are not about the obvious functions often associated with pottery; they function in our lives as objects of beauty.

may's lick

STUDIO HOURS	BY APPOINTMENT
SHOWROOM	YES
HOURS	BY APPOINTMENT
WORK IS SOLD	RETAIL/WHOLESALE

selected kentucky galleries

Piedmont Gallery, Augusta

Contemporary Artifacts Gallery, Berea

The White Gallery, Maysville

DIRECTIONS
2.5 miles west of May's Lick off Rte. 324.

STUDIO NAME
Seigel Pottery
STUDIO ADDRESS
2545 Hwy. 127-S
Owenton, KY   40359
(502) 484-2970
gseigel@kih.net

20

greg seigel

Greg Seigel studied sociology at the University of Cincinnati from 1965 to 1969 and at Ohio State University from 1969 to 1970. In 1971 he began to teach himself various pottery techniques such as throwing, hand building, glazing, kiln building, and firing. He has extensive experience teaching ceramics to children through the Artist-in-the-Schools Program and has worked in more than 25 schools throughout the state. Seigel has exhibited his work in a variety of galleries in the region dating back to 1974. His work has been featured in the book *Kentucky Crafts: Handmade and Heartfelt* by Phyllis George (New York: Crown Publishers, 1989), and he was the recipient of an Early Times Scholarship in 1992. He owns and operates Seigel Pottery in Owenton and continues to sell his pottery in a variety of art galleries and shops throughout the region, as well as through his studio.

Seigel's pottery is all high-fired stoneware made from a blend of local and regional clays and fired in gas and wood kilns. Most of the ware is functional (teapots, casseroles, vases, covered jars, etc.) and often exhibits a sense of humor, while some work is purely sculptural and almost always humorous. His concern and love for handmade pottery is evident in his work, and the playful nature of the pieces he makes provides testimony for this love. Having useful pieces of pottery to use in the home is, for Seigel, the completion of the working process in clay. While earning a living is an important aspect for any production potter living on work, Seigel has found a way to balance the difficulty of making money with the freedom to investigate new ideas.

about the artist

owenton

STUDIO HOURS	BY APPOINTMENT
SHOWROOM	YES
HOURS	BY APPOINTMENT
WORK IS SOLD	RETAIL/WHOLESALE

selected kentucky galleries

Capital Gallery, Frankfort

Kentucky Art and Craft Foundation, Louisville

Promenade Gallery, Berea

DIRECTIONS

Two miles south of Owenton on Rte. 127-S.

The Daniel Boone National Forest runs through much of the area known as the Highlands, and this easternmost edge of the state is best known as the craft capital of Kentucky. A mountainous region with lakes and hollows, the Highland area of eastern Kentucky provides a unique look into one aspect of Kentucky culture and life.

highlands region

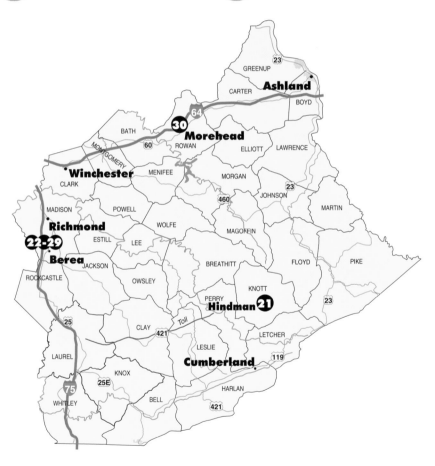

It is in this region that you will easily encounter traditional artisans working in wood and fiber. You will also see working craft cooperatives such as Appalshop in Whitesburg that encourage the preservation and sharing of information and techniques. Other notable craft centers such as the Kentucky Folk Art Center in Morehead serve to preserve and promote the region's folk art. Music, dance, and craft traditions all share a piece of the cultural pie that helps define this region.

The area also supports a variety of fairs and festivals meant to market the culture and educate the consumer about mountain life. Berea, a unique folk arts and crafts center, boasts the well-known Berea College Crafts Apprenticeship program and the Kentucky Guild of Artists and Craftsmen and is ideal for locating some of the mountains' best artisans through several of the town's galleries and shops. Other academic centers such as Eastern Kentucky University in Richmond and Morehead State University in Morehead serve to provide ample facilities and training for many of the younger artists from the Highlands.

The ceramics in the Highlands Region is curious only in the number of artists working in clay. While other craft traditions have enjoyed a rich history with a large number of artists working in various mediums such as wood and fiber, this has not been the case for ceramics in the mountains. However, this is not to suggest that those working in the Highlands Region of the state are at a disadvantage. The ceramists listed in this book continue to produce some of the finest clay work from across the state.

STUDIO NAME
Michael Ware Pottery
STUDIO ADDRESS
Hindman Settlement School
Hindman, KY 41822
(606) 785-5053
(606) 785-5475
mikeware9@hotmail.com

michael ware

Michael Ware received a bachelor's degree in art education from Millersville University in Millersville, Pennsylvania, in 1974 and a master's degree from Morehead State University in Morehead in 1987. He is currently on the faculty at Alice Lloyd College in Pippa Passes, where he has taught art since 1992. In addition, he is an adjunct faculty member at the Hazard Community College evening art program and at the Hindman Settlement School in Hindman. He is a member of the Kentucky Crafts Marketing program and is active in the arts community in and around Hindman.

Ware has been a production potter for over 21 years and, during this time, has steadily produced a wide variety of utilitarian forms. He currently works in stoneware, which is fired in electric kilns; however, his background in production pottery includes a variety of techniques, including salt-glazed ceramics. Because of his love for Pennsylvania Dutch salt-glazed pottery, he developed a self-glazing clay body that has the appearance of the salt-glazing effects, one that he plans to use in his line of utilitarian pieces. Ware has developed various clay bodies and glazes for his line of pottery and frequently carves and pierces designs into his work, creating a wide array of graphic effects. His work is direct in appearance with rich, textural surfaces that add a quiet sophistication to the overall forms.

about the artist

hindman

STUDIO HOURS	BY APPOINTMENT
SHOWROOM	YES
HOURS	MONDAY-FRIDAY 10 AM-4 PM SATURDAY 10 AM-3 PM
WORK IS SOLD	RETAIL/WHOLESALE

DIRECTIONS
Take the London Exit (D.B. Pkwy.) off I-75. Go east toward Manchester and Hazard. Road turns into Rt. 80 at Hazard. Stay on road until Hindman Settlement School. Turn off at Rt. 160. Take this road into Hindman and follow signs for the Hindman Settlement School.

selected kentucky galleries

Marie Stewart Crafts Cabin, Hindman

STUDIO NAME
Cedar Meadow Studios
STUDIO ADDRESS
244 Wolf Gap Road
Berea, KY 40403
(859) 986-2432

28 N. Broadway
Old Town, Berea, KY

teresa cole

Teresa Cole received her ceramics training from 1970 to 1972 while serving as an apprentice through the Berea College Ceramics Apprenticeship Program. She later went on to complete a bachelor's degree at Berea College in 1973. She has attended numerous ceramics workshops over the years and remains active in a variety of local arts organizations. She has been an exhibiting member of the Kentucky Guild of Artists and Craftsmen since 1974 and has served on various KGAC committees. She is a founding member of the Berea Craftspersons Association and served as its chairperson from 1983 to 1987. In addition, she has been a member of the Berea Arts Council since 1987 and the Lexington Art League since 1985, and has been an exhibiting member of the Kentucky Art and Craft Foundation in Louisville. Cole has exhibited her ceramic works steadily since 1975 and has been featured in various notable publications such as *Studio Potter Magazine* and *Ceramics Monthly*.

Cole's ceramic work is primarily functional ceramic tableware fired to midrange stoneware temperatures. She often leaves the clay body exposed (unglazed) with slip-trailed decoration. She uses engobes (slips) and terra sigillata for colored surfaces. The warmth of these surface treatments adds greatly to her desired effect of creating pottery forms that are close to the earth in tone. Cole also frequently works with other potters in the Berea community to fire raku- and wood-fired kilns.

Her work is inspired mostly by nature, so she tries to create form and surface effects that allow viewers to fill in the details with their own experiences in the natural world. Cole said, "It seems I am as impressed by the shadow of a leaf floating in a pool in the stream as I am by the sunset over the Pacific, so I record the more subtle, intimately experienced aspects of my environment." Cole, who lives in rural Kentucky, attempts to blend her lifestyle and her concern for nature with her love of creating objects in clay.

about the artist

berea

STUDIO HOURS	MONDAY-THURSDAY BY APPOINTMENT
SHOWROOM	YES
HOURS	MONDAY-SATURDAY 10 AM-5 PM
WORK IS SOLD	RETAIL/WHOLESALE

selected kentucky galleries

Kentucky Art and Craft Foundation, Louisville

Upstairs Gallery, Berea

Marie Stewart Craft Gallery, Hindman

DIRECTIONS

From Boone Tavern in Berea, take Rt. 21 east to Bighill, go left onto U.S. 421 north 1 1/4 miles. Right onto Rt. 594 (Red Lick Road), go 3.2 miles, left onto Wolf Gap Road. Go 3/4 miles, right at private gravel drive marked Tater Knob Pottery, drive past pottery, crest hill, continue through the woods to a drive at flagpole on left. Turn there and drive up the hill to studio.

STUDIO NAME
Tater Knob Pottery
and Farm
STUDIO ADDRESS
260 Wolf Gap Road
Berea, KY   40403
(859) 986-2167

sarah culbreth/jeff enge

Sarah Culbreth and Jeff Enge graduated from Berea College with their bachelor's degrees in art and worked in the college's apprenticeship program. Together they own and operate the Tater Knob Pottery, which was founded in 1992, and is located just outside of Berea.

Sarah Culbreth's ceramics experience goes back to 1976 and includes working as an assistant to David Leach at Berea College in 1978. She has worked extensively with small children at various workshops from 1983 to 1993 and co-owned the private pottery Studio 105 from 1980 to 1992. An active member of the Berea community, Culbreth has been involved with the Berea Arts Council, the Berea Craftsperson's Association (BCA), the Chamber of Commerce, and the Berea Business and Professional Women's Club.

Jeff Enge's ceramic work began in the early 1980s when he worked as a hand painter for Haager Pottery in Illinois. He has worked as an apprentice in Wisconsin and as an assistant at Studio 105. He was the owner of Stonewall Pottery in Berea for two years before joining forces with Culbreth and starting the Tater Knob Pottery.

Tater Knob Pottery, located in the foothills of the Cumberland Mountains, produces a line of over 100 items, including dinnerware settings, pitchers, vases, lamps, bells, and the popular Spoon Bread Baker, designed to bake and serve the spoon bread specialty made famous by the Boone Tavern Hotel in Berea. The pieces are hand thrown with red clay, then high-fired to a strong finish. All of the work is completed using lead-free glazes in an array of subtle colors, and it is all oven-, microwave-, and dishwasher-safe. The simplicity of form and surface reflects the natural beauty of the wooded acres on Wolf Gap Road, where the pottery is located.

Culbreth and Enge's work is sold extensively in shops and galleries throughout Kentucky and at several outdoor shows, including the Kentucky Guild of Artists and Craftsmen's fairs held twice annually in Berea. The variety of utilitarian forms produced by the potters of Tater Knob is extensive and meets the many needs of the local and tourist markets.

berea

STUDIO HOURS	MONDAY-SATURDAY 9 AM-5 PM
SHOWROOM	YES
HOURS	MONDAY-SATURDAY 9 AM-5 PM
WORK IS SOLD	RETAIL/WHOLESALE

selected kentucky galleries

Loghouse Craft Gallery, Berea

Boone Tavern Gift Shop, Berea

Various State Park Gift Shops

DIRECTIONS

From downtown Berea, take Hwy. 21 to Rt. 421, turn left. Take Rt. 421 approximately 1 mile. Turn right on Rt. 594 and go approximately 3.5 miles. You will pass over 3 concrete bridges. Wolf Gap Road turns only to the left about 1/2 mile from the last bridge. Turn left on Wolf Gap Road. Tater Knob Pottery is about 1/2 mile from the creek on the right.

STUDIO NAME
Artifacts Pottery
STUDIO ADDRESS
327 Chestnut St.
Berea, KY   40403
(859) 986-1096
e-mail and/or web site.

25

gwen heffner

Gwen Heffner received a bachelor's degree in printmaking and ceramics from Luther College in Decorah, Iowa, in 1976 and a master's degree in ceramics from the University of Louisville in 1978. She has exhibited her artwork in the region regularly throughout the years and has received several prestigious awards, including an Al Smith Fellowship in 2000 from the Kentucky Arts Council and two Early Times Scholarships in 1994 and 2000. She has conducted workshops and written articles on ceramics and has had her work featured in a number of major ceramic art publications. She remains active in a number of professional organizations, such as the American Craft Council, the Kentucky Guild of Artists and Craftsmen, the Ohio Designer Craftsmen, and the Southern Highland Handicraft Guild. Her work is part of the Ceramics Monthly permanent collection; the collection of the International Ceramics Museum at Alfred, New York; and other significant ceramic art collections. She has sold her work steadily over the years in art galleries, shops, and fairs throughout the region. She began working independently as a studio potter in 1981 and has owned Contemporary Artifacts Gallery in Berea since 1992.

Heffner makes a line of functional dinnerware that is slip-trailed. She also produces a line of vessels with altered and carved rims made of pure white clay. All of her work is made from porcelain clay high-fired to over 2,000 degrees Fahrenheit. Her work is generally oxidation-fired in electric kilns, with some pieces fired in reduction and wood-fired atmospheres.

Gwen Heffner's work is largely inspired by forms such as shells, rocks, and flowers, which find their way into her design through the gentle manipulation and altering of her vessels. The smooth, clean, porcelain skins on her pieces reflect the surfaces of beach rocks, eggshells, and other sensuous coverings, while the whiteness of the clay provides her a canvas on which to explore these varied finishes. Her success at creating beautiful and useful ceramic forms serves as a reminder of the importance of objects that serve as vehicles for communication between makers and users.

about the artist

berea

STUDIO HOURS	10 AM-5 PM DAILY
SHOWROOM	YES
HOURS	11 AM-5 PM (closed on Sunday)
WORK IS SOLD	RETAIL/WHOLESALE

selected kentucky galleries

Images Friedman Gallery, Louisville

Kentucky Art and Craft Foundation, Louisville

Appalachian Fireside Gallery, Berea

Contemporary Artifacts Gallery, Berea

David Appalachian Crafts, David

DIRECTIONS

Take exit 76 off I-75 and travel east into Berea on Rt. 21, which becomes Chestnut Street. The studio and gallery are located on the right immediately after the third stoplight intersection. Parking is in front of the gallery or along the street.

STUDIO NAME
Walter Hyleck
STUDIO ADDRESS
3477 Scaffold Cane Road
Berea, KY   40403
(859) 986-3463
hyleck@berea.edu

26

walter hyleck

Walter Hyleck received his bachelor's degree in 1965 from the University of Minnesota in Duluth. He completed a master of fine arts degree in ceramics and art history from Tulane University in New Orleans, Louisiana, in 1967. He has taught full time at Berea College since 1967 and served as chair of the department from 1984 to 1996. He has been the director of the Ceramic Apprenticeship Program from 1971 to 1995 and again from 1996 to the present. He was also a visiting professor at the University of Minnesota during the summer of 1974.

Hyleck's career is marked by numerous awards, including an Al Smith Fellowship from the Kentucky Arts Council. He has exhibited his artwork nationally in one-person and group shows dating back to 1966. His work is represented in some of the finest collections across the country and has been shown in a variety of magazines and books.

Walter Hyleck's work in clay is divided between functional tableware and nonfunctional ceramic sculpture. The work is often in porcelain, both oxidation- and reduction-fired to temperatures well over 2,000 degrees Fahrenheit. He also produces pieces made of red and black earthenware fired to a medium range of approximately 2,000 degrees. While most of his work is wheel-thrown, he also combines various slip-casting and hand-forming techniques in the making of his pieces. In more recent pieces he has used a mixed-media approach that combines slate and clay. All of these techniques continue to push his understanding of how sculptural objects maintain a vessel reference. Whether he creates teapots, bowls, or sculptural fountains, Hyleck's work is always on the cutting edge of ceramics and its relationship to contemporary life. His work has been extremely consistent throughout his career in clay and has added greatly to the high standards of clay work often associated with contemporary ceramics in Kentucky and beyond.

about the artist

STUDIO HOURS	BY APPOINTMENT
SHOWROOM	NO
HOURS	N/A
WORK IS SOLD	RETAIL/WHOLESALE

selected kentucky galleries

Kentucky Art and Craft Foundation, Louisville

Images Friedman Gallery, Louisville

DIRECTIONS
Call for directions.

STUDIO NAME
Martin Studio
STUDIO ADDRESS
311 Wolf Gap Rd.
Berea, KY   40403
(859) 986-9205
jr_martin3@yahoo.com
www.artisans-america.com/pots

john martin

John Martin, a native of Western Kentucky, received his bachelor of fine arts degree from Western Kentucky University in 1986 and his master of fine arts degree from Southern Illinois University at Carbondale in 1989. John, together with his wife, Sue, a fiber artist, began the Martin Studio in Berea in 1990. The couple's work is sold at art fairs and galleries across the country as well as at their own studio. He has received numerous awards throughout the Midwest for his unique raku ceramic work and has taught people of all ages at public demonstrations and community classes. He recently began teaching studio art as an adjunct faculty member at Eastern Kentucky University in Richmond. Martin is active with local and state craft organizations, such as the Berea Craftspersons Association, which he served as president from 1995 to 1996; the Kentucky Guild of Artists and Craftsmen; and Paducah Clay.

Martin is best known for his innovative styles in porcelain and raku. He has developed special clay and glaze effects using materials from his rural property that give his work a unique and personal appearance. His line of pottery encompasses wheel-thrown utilitarian ware as well as more sculptural hand-built forms that often use the figure as a point of reference. Colorful raku surfaces with gold lusters for accents are trademarks of his personal style.

In addition, he continues to investigate new and fresh forms and has created a line of work that is fired entirely with wood. Utilizing the soft marks of the flame and ash, Martin has expanded upon his offerings by creating pieces that contrast favorably with the bolder coloration of raku.

about the artist

berea

STUDIO HOURS	BY APPOINTMENT
SHOWROOM	NO
HOURS	N/A
WORK IS SOLD	RETAIL/WHOLESALE

selected kentucky galleries

Promenade Gallery, Berea

Kentucky Art and Craft Foundation, Louisville

Louisville Visual Arts Association, Louisville

Artifacts Gallery, Bowling Green

Artique, Lexington

Marcum's, Louisville

Bebe's Artisan Market, Paducah

DIRECTIONS

From Berea take Rt. 21 (Boone Tavern) past Indian Fort Theater. Take a left at the end of Rt. 21 onto Rt. 421. Go one mile on Rt. 421, take a right on Rt. 594 (Red Lick Road). Go 3.5 miles on Rt. 594. Take a left on Wolf Gap Road. Pottery is located one mile on left.

28

STUDIO NAME
Berea College Pottery
STUDIO ADDRESS
Danforth Building
Berea College
Berea, KY 40403
(859) 985-3231
trent_ripley@berea.edu
www.geocities.com/SoHo/2210

trent ripley

Trent Ripley received a bachelor's degree from Indiana University in Bloomington in 1991 and a master of fine arts degree from Kent State University in Kent, Ohio, in 1993. He has worked as a studio assistant at the Penland School of Crafts in Penland, North Carolina, and as a ceramics instructor at the John Waldon Center in Bloomington, Indiana. Currently, he is the resident potter at Berea College, where he has worked since 1994. Ripley has mentored students in the Ceramics Apprenticeship Program, produced a line of wares for sale by the college, and coordinated studio operations, as well as maintained a personal line of pottery. He has exhibited his pottery regularly throughout the region dating back to 1990 and sells his work through a variety of galleries and shops across the state.

Ripley's work is mostly functional stoneware pieces fired in either reduction or wood-firing atmospheres. Functional forms such as bottles, oval bowls, lidded jars, and even ceramic drums are only part of the variety of utilitarian forms he creates. His interest in the functional aspects of pottery is always evident in his work. Attention is given to the immediacy of forms and how they can be quickly produced while still maintaining a strong focus on utility. Simple surface treatments that take full advantage of his firing processes serve to strengthen the directness of the forms. His desire to produce pieces that can be easily transferred from maker to user is apparent, and this aspect of his pottery production remains a vital concern for him and for his work. Ripley said, "Making functional pots allows me to indulge my creative urges while producing useful and attractive objects that can be shared and enjoyed by others. . . . The utility and accessibility of the pots is therefore fundamentally important to me; the work must be passed on and used, or the efforts are merely self-indulgent exercises."

about the artist

berea

STUDIO HOURS	8 AM-5 PM
SHOWROOM	NO
HOURS	N/A
WORK IS SOLD	RETAIL/WHOLESALE

selected kentucky galleries

Log House Gallery, Berea

Boone Tavern Gift Shop, Berea

Kentucky Art and Craft Foundation, Lousiville

DIRECTIONS

Take exit 595 into Berea. Go through first traffic light, take first right (Campus Drive), bear left at first divide. Look for kiln chimney on left. Pottery is in the basement of Danforth Industrial Building.

STUDIO NAME
J. Wright Pottery and Metal
STUDIO ADDRESS
1598 Boonesborough Road
Richmond, KY   40475
(859) 623-7777

james wright

James Wright, a native of Murphysboro, Illinois, received his bachelor of fine arts degree in industrial design from the University of Illinois in 1961. From 1961 to 1963, he served as the military base crafts director at Manzano Base in Albuquerque, New Mexico. In 1965 he earned a master of fine arts degree in ceramics and jewelry from Southern Illinois University. From 1965 to 1968, he was an art instructor at General Beadle State College (now Dakota State University) in Madison, South Dakota; from 1968 to 1969, a visiting professor of art at the University of Evansville, Indiana; and from 1969 to 1973, an assistant professor of art at Eastern Kentucky University. In 1973, along with his wife, Nancy, he opened J. Wright Pottery and Metal in Richmond, which they still operate today. In addition to working on commission, he sells work at his studio and through various galleries and shops throughout the state.

James Wright's ceramic work is both functional and decorative stoneware. Utilitarian pieces reflect his desire to create forms that fit into the home. The pottery also produces hand-built pieces as well as porcelain and Egyptian paste jewelry, most of these coming from Nancy Wright. Together, the Wrights create a wide range of forms that address practical utilitarian and decorative needs and delicate accessories for body adornment.

about the artist

rich mond

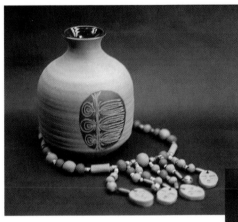

STUDIO HOURS	9 AM-5 PM
SHOWROOM	NO
HOURS	N/A
WORK IS SOLD	RETAIL/WHOLESALE

selected kentucky galleries

Log House Gallery, Berea

Various State Park Gift Shops

Bebe's Artisan Market, Paducah

DIRECTIONS

Take the Boonesboro exit off I-75 and go east. The pottery is ahead about 1/2 mile on the left.

STUDIO NAME
The Flophouse Pottery
STUDIO ADDRESS
125 S. Wilson
Morehead, KY   40351
(606) 784-8483

tom reitz

Tom Reitz began his career in clay while a student at Morehead State University, where he received a bachelor's degree in university studies in 1984. By taking ceramics classes as an elective, he soon discovered a love for a process and a material that lead him to a lifelong career as a production potter.

Reitz shows his work regularly throughout the region in a variety of craft venues and is an active participant with the Kentucky Craft Marketing Program. A native of Owensboro who has lived in Morehead since 1979, Reitz owns and operates the successful Flophouse Pottery.

Tom Reitz produces a line of utilitarian pottery fired in electric kilns to stoneware temperatures. The clay, which he digs himself, all comes from the nearby Clack Mountain clay vein. Some of the many functional forms he produces are mugs, bowls, baking dishes, cream and sugar sets, and honey pots. Commissioned and special-order pieces are also part of the wide inventory of clay forms made at his pottery. His interest in utilitarian forms and traditional pottery techniques is evident in the line produced at Flophouse Pottery, especially seen through his use and understanding of bold forms marked with simple glaze decorations. Reitz said, "The rewards for me are producing things that people use and enjoy using." It is this basic need that has kept the Flophouse Pottery producing forms that find their way into the homes of consumers throughout the Kentucky region and beyond.

morehead

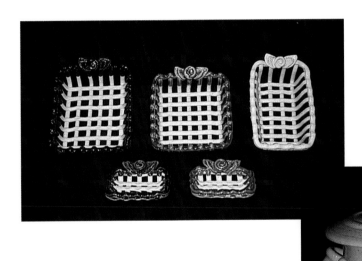

STUDIO HOURS	10 AM-5 PM
SHOWROOM	YES
HOURS	10 AM-5 PM
WORK IS SOLD	RETAIL/WHOLESALE

selected kentucky galleries

Various State Park Gift Shops

DIRECTIONS
From I-64 take U.S. 32 into Morehead. Take a left on Main St. Go through a four-way stop and take the next right onto S. Wilson.

Known to many as the scenic wonderlands of Kentucky, the Cumberland Region is known for the world's longest cave system, Mammoth Cave. The region also boasts the famous Cumberland Falls, complete with the popular moonbow, and two of the state's finest lakes. A true outdoor paradise, the Cumberland area is rich in beautiful natural geography, where visitors can regularly explore, play, and enjoy nature at its best.

cumberland region

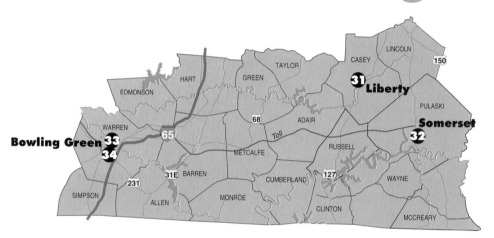

While the area is mostly rural, the region's two main cities of Somerset and Bowling Green are situated at opposite edges from east to west within the region. Located in the city of Bowling Green, Western Kentucky University provides ample opportunity for training artists as well as venues for viewing contemporary and traditional art. Here one finds the Kentucky Museum, where the focus is on Kentucky history and culture.

In the Cumberland Region, there are few artists making a living in ceramics, yet they still manage to maintain a high standard of pottery production. The main support for these traditions has come primarily through Western Kentucky University Art Department, where ceramics has been nurtured for years. The program has enabled those interested in clay work to develop in the healthy environment of the art department. For the most part, those working in ceramics in this region continue to run successful pottery studios that focus on serving the utilitarian needs of users.

about the region

STUDIO NAME
Woodscreek Pottery
STUDIO ADDRESS
2932 Woodscreek Road
Liberty, KY   42539
(606) 787-7965

31

davie reneau

Davie Reneau studied art at Western Kentucky University, where she received her bachelor of fine arts degree in 1985. She continued her education at West Virginia University, where she completed a master of fine arts degree in 1995. She taught part time at Western Kentucky University from 1995 to 1996, Campbellsville University in 1996 and 1998, and Eastern Kentucky University in 1998. She also served as a studio assistant at the Arrowmont School of Arts and Crafts in Gatlinburg, Tennessee, in 1992 and 1993. In 1995 she opened Woodscreek Pottery in Liberty, which she still operates.

Reneau has exhibited her work regionally since the mid-1990s and has received several awards for her ceramics, including a Kentucky Arts Council Al Smith Fellowship in 2000 and an Early Times Scholarship in 1999. She sells her work in local and regional galleries and shops and has given various lectures and workshops in the area.

Reneau's pottery is all wheel-thrown, wood-fired utilitarian ware, functional pieces meant for everyday use within the home. Covered jars, teapots, vases, and pitchers are the main focus of her line, with vase forms the most recent emphasis in her work. While these pieces retain a functional aesthetic, they are now made to take on the full effect of the wood-firing process. According to Reneau, "The pots (vases) are thrown with the same directness and sensibilities as my functional work and have greatly affected my other pots, but they are directed toward visual satisfaction rather than utilitarian or tactile satisfaction." These newer vase forms are more about the firing process and how wood ash and flame help to define and articulate the visual qualities of each piece. The use of visual elements is all part of the search to discover and to make beautiful utilitarian pieces fired with wood.

liberty

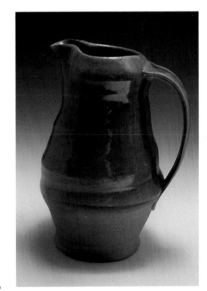

STUDIO HOURS	BY APPOINTMENT
SHOWROOM	NO
HOURS	N/A
WORK IS SOLD	RETAIL/WHOLESALE

selected kentucky galleries

Contemporary Artifacts Gallery, Berea

Kentucky Art and Craft Foundation, Louisville

Swanson Cralle Gallery, Louisville

Lill Street Gallery, Chicago

DIRECTIONS

127 South from Danville, turn onto Hwy. 70 (headed toward Campbellsville). Turn at Clementsville Road (across from Frank's Food Mart.) Turn on 1st road on right (Woodscreek Road). Look for blue mailbox, driveway on left.

STUDIO NAME
Fire and Clay Pottery
STUDIO ADDRESS
2535 Pumphouse Road
Somerset, KY 42503
(606) 679-7897
meg@megpots.com
John@megpots.com
www.megpots.com

meg mcclorey

Meriwether "Meg" McClorey received her bachelor of science degree in design from the University of Cincinnati in 1974. She continued her interest in ceramics throughout the 1970s and 1980s, taking classes and workshops at a number of notable institutions, such as Arrowmont School of Arts and Crafts in Gatlinburg, Tennessee; Penland School of Crafts in Penland, North Carolina; Santa Barbara Art Institute; and the University of Kentucky. She has taught at a variety of locations throughout the state, has served as an artist-in-residence for the Watershed Arts Alliance from 1994 to 1996, and has taught pottery at Somerset Community College's Continuing Education program. She has exhibited her work dating back to 1980 and has participated in art shows sponsored by the Kentucky Guild of Artists and Craftsmen, of which she is a member. With her husband, John, she is co-owner of Fire and Clay Pottery, which they began in 1979.

McClorey's pottery line is a combination of raku, stoneware, and porcelain, all with a primary focus on utilitarian wares. Other forms with a more sculptural emphasis produced at Fire and Clay are hand-built and/or thrown. Stoneware and porcelain forms are fired in an electric kiln with an oxidizing atmosphere, while the raku pieces are all fired with gas. The various firing techniques and processes allow the artist to create unique visual effects that help define the particular line of pottery. Pieces are often glazed white or clear to allow for a clean base onto which colorful brushwork can be applied. McClorey seeks utility within the home for most of what she produces at the pottery.

somerset

STUDIO HOURS	1-4 PM WEEKDAYS
SHOWROOM	YES
HOURS	1-4 PM WEEKDAYS
WORK IS SOLD	RETAIL/WHOLESALE

selected kentucky galleries

Kentucky Art and Craft Foundation, Louisville

Pinecone Primitives, Somerset

DIRECTIONS
From Hwy. 80, east of Somerset and the intersection of Hwy. 461, drive west on Hwy. 80 for 4.25 miles to Rte. 3260 – Pumphouse Road. Turn right onto Rte. 3260 and drive about 7/10 mile to Fire and Clay on the right. From Somerset, or the intersection of Hwys. 80 and 27, drive east on Hwy. 80 bypass to Rte. 3260 – Pumphouse Road. Turn left onto Rte. 3260 and drive about 2.7 miles miles to Fire and Clay located on the left.

STUDIO NAME
Rickman Pottery
STUDIO ADDRESS
1121 E. 14th Ave.
Bowling Green, KY
42104
(270) 782-8550

mitchell rickman

Mitchell Rickman began his career in clay while studying at Western Kentucky University, where he received a bachelor's degree in sociology in 1983. It was here studying with Bill Weaver that he took elective courses in ceramics and soon discovered a love for the material and functional pottery. He later went on to work at the Overcast Pottery in Nashville, Tennessee, from 1986 to 1990 before returning to Bowling Green, where he currently owns and operates Rickman Pottery.

An active member of the Kentucky Crafts Marketing Program, Rickman sells his work regularly throughout the region at various craft venues and has received several awards.

Rickman's pottery is primarily wheel-thrown functional dinnerware and accessories. Casseroles, teapots, vases, and other utilitarian items are all high-fired in electric kilns and decorated with a variety of glaze surfaces and colors that employ a wide array of traditional and contemporary patterns. An attention to domestic pottery and its role in our lives is apparent in the items Rickman produces, yet decorative pieces also find their place within the repertoire of forms he produces. Work that is primarily meant for daily life remains the driving force behind the pottery made at Rickman Pottery in Bowling Green.

about the artist

bowling green

STUDIO HOURS	MONDAY-SATURDAY 10 AM-6 PM
SHOWROOM	YES
HOURS	MONDAY-SATURDAY 10 AM-6 PM
WORK IS SOLD	RETAIL/WHOLESALE

selected kentucky galleries

Kentucky State Park Gift Shops

Completely Kentucky, Frankfort

True Kentucky, Glendale

Kentucky Haus, Newport

DIRECTIONS

From I-65, take exit 22, Rte. 231 north into Bowling Green, approximately 3.5 miles. Left at light onto 31-W south. Go 2 blocks to light. Left on 14th Ave. Rickman Pottery is 1/2 block on right.

STUDIO NAME
Malcolm Mobutu
STUDIO ADDRESS
Western Kentucky University
Department of Art
1 Big Red Way
Bowling Green, KY   42101-3576
(270) 745-5886
malcolm.smith@wku.edu
www.geocities.com/soho/studios/8847/

malcolm mobutu smith

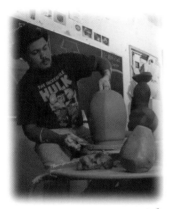

MOBUTU

Malcolm Mobutu Smith studied ceramics at Kansas City Art Institute from 1988 to 1989 and received a bachelor of fine arts degree from Pennsylvania State University in 1994. He earned his master of fine arts degree from New York State College of Ceramics at Alfred University in 1996. Smith has exhibited his ceramic artwork regularly dating back to 1987. He has received numerous awards and has pieces in several collections, including those of Trans Financial Bank in Bowling Green; the International Museum of Ceramics in Alfred, New York; the Jingdezhen Institute of Fine Art in Jingdezhen, China; and Baker University in Baldwin, Kansas. He is represented by galleries in Massachusetts, Pennsylvania, and Illinois. He is regularly asked to conduct workshops and give lectures on his artwork and was recently featured in a cover story for *Ceramics: Art and Perception* magazine pages 3-6 (Sydney, Australia, #30, 1997).

Smith's ceramic work is mostly thrown and hand-built vessels that are altered. He uses earthenware clays with terra sigillata or glazed surfaces or stoneware with glaze. His work bridges cultural gaps within geographic boundaries and within the very nature of art and craft. While his work often takes on a playful, cartoon characteristic, it also pushes the limits between two- and three-dimensional art. His pieces are far more than pots, yet it is the very nature of ceramics that inspires and motivates him to create vessels of meaning and purpose. Smith said, "Form, this inner body, is fleshed out by my interest in jazz internalization, the subcultures of hip-hop's expressiveness, and an awareness of my multiethnicity within the art world." His work is a type of narrative, but it is still about ceramics, decoration, and art, as well as culture and life.

about the artist

bowling green

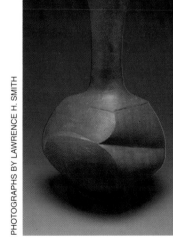

PHOTOGRAPHS BY LAWRENCE H. SMITH

STUDIO HOURS	BY APPOINTMENT
SHOWROOM	NO
HOURS	N/A
WORK IS SOLD	RETAIL

selected kentucky galleries

DIRECTIONS
Call for directions.

Western Kentucky is best known for its famous Land between the Lakes, a 170,000-acre peninsula surrounded by Lake Barkley and Kentucky Lake. A true outdoor paradise, the western edge of the state is vast in its sky and spacious in geography. Bordered on the west by the mighty Mississippi and on the north by the Ohio River, the Western Lakes Region is a sharp contrast to the rolling hills of the eastern slopes of the state.

western lakes region

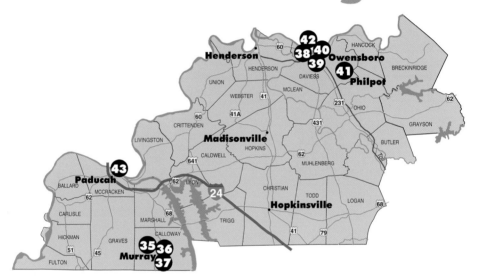

With historic river cities like Paducah and Owensboro, a special charm is always in the air. Bluegrass music festivals, art fairs, barbecue, and the American Quilter's Society Museum are no small part of this city's special place within the state.

Academic centers in Murray (Murray State University) and Owensboro (Brescia College) provide training in the ceramic arts. In addition, the Clara M. Eagle Gallery at Murray State University and the Owensboro Museum of Fine Arts regularly display a wide array of traditional and contemporary art and craft from the state and the region.

The work of ceramic artists from the Western Lakes Region is another example of the high quality of contemporary ceramic work produced across Kentucky. Functional and sculptural ceramics are both evident in this region, and an appreciation of current clay trends is visible. While small in number relative to the larger areas of the state, the clay workers of the Western Lakes Region continue to produce and promote their work in Kentucky and beyond.

STUDIO NAME
Blood River Studio
STUDIO ADDRESS
8332 Rte. 121 South
Murray, KY   42071
(270) 436-5610

wayne l. bates

about the artist

Wayne Bates, a native of Georgia, earned a bachelor's degree from Union University in Jackson, Tennessee, in 1965. He went on to earn a master of fine arts degree in ceramics at the University of Georgia in Athens in 1970. While working as kiln supervisor at the Haystack School of Crafts in Maine, he met noted ceramist William Daley, who later hired him to teach at the Philadelphia College of Art, where he remained for eight years (1970-78). During this time he also served as ceramics consultant for the Moravian Tile Works in nearby Doylestown, where he supervised the reactivation of tile production. He gave up academia and urban life and moved to Western Kentucky in 1978, where he began his career as a full-time production potter. He has exhibited his work nationally dating back to 1973 and has received numerous awards, including an Al Smith Fellowship from the Kentucky Arts Council in 1988. Bates now owns and operates the Blood River Studio in Murray and sells his work through various galleries and shops throughout the region.

Bates produces a variety of thrown forms using commercially prepared, translucent cone 6 porcelain. Forms are coated while wet (leather-hard) with a colored engobe (clay slip), which is then carved into the surface using the sgraffito technique. The designs carved into the surfaces of bowls, platters, and vases add greatly to the forms, with the engobes enhancing the finished pieces. A clear (translucent) glaze is usually applied to the final form before glaze firing, which allows a wide range of colors to shine through, although Bates sometimes uses a matte glaze on the carved surface of the engobe to alter the appearance of the design.

A fascination with carved designs that reflect a multitude of variations and permutations steers his artistic vision of surface on form. Pieces that work much like paintings, yet reflect the traditions of pottery, are trademarks of his personal style. He claims that his work is more about intellect and less about emotions and feelings. He, therefore, looks at each piece as part of a continuum of the production process, each piece influenced in part by the one before it. The repetition and order of producing similar forms in a production environment suits Bates's aesthetics and steers his work into an endless array of possibilities.

murray

STUDIO HOURS	BY APPOINTMENT
SHOWROOM	YES
HOURS	BY APPOINTMENT
WORK IS SOLD	RETAIL/WHOLESALE

selected kentucky galleries

Kentucky Art and Craft Foundation, Louisville

Museum of the American Quilters Society, Paducah

DIRECTIONS

From Murray, follow Hwy. 121 south 8 miles to a sign with my name at a driveway. Turn left and follow signs to studio/gallery.

STUDIO NAME
Susan O'Brien
STUDIO ADDRESS
57 Rayburn Road
Murray, KY   42071
(270) 435-4460
susan.obrien@murraystate.edu

susan o'brien

Susan O'Brien received a bachelor of fine arts degree in sculpture and a bachelor of science degree in psychology from the University of Tennessee in Chattanooga in 1986. She studied ceramics at the University of Colorado from 1992 to 1994, the Nova Scotia College of Art and Design from 1994 to 1995, and Louisiana State University from 1995 to 1998, where she completed her master of fine arts degree. She has exhibited her work in several prestigious exhibitions throughout the United States, including the NCECA National Clay Exhibition in Columbus, Ohio; the Strictly Functional Exhibit in Ephrata, Pennsylvania; and the Orton Cone Box Show in Baldwin, Kansas. She was a resident at the Archie Bray Foundation in Montana in 1998 and has had work published in *Ceramics Monthly* and *The Best of Pottery II* (Gloucester, Mass.: Rockport Publishers, 1998). She is currently on the faculty at Murray State University, where she teaches ceramics.

O'Brien's ceramic work is high-temperature white stoneware fired in oxidation kilns. Pieces consist primarily of coffeepots, teapots, salt-and-pepper sets, butter dishes, fruit bowls, and a variety of other functional forms meant for the table. Her work is inspired by 18th-century silver, Turkish ceramics, and Fabergé eggs, all carefully woven together with a sense of playfulness and subtle irreverence.

Ornamentation and decoration are trademarks of O'Brien's ceramics; beautifully orchestrated details of form and surface express a nostalgia for craftsmanship and an intrigue for utility. She said, "As I work, a dialogue emerges between my pots and my thoughts. I weave various layers of textural and decorative information, provoking intrigue for both the viewer and myself." O'Brien's pieces primarily address issues of function but are also statements of human interaction through the daily use of ceramic objects.

about the artist

murray

STUDIO HOURS	BY APPOINTMENT
SHOWROOM	NO
HOURS	N/A
WORK IS SOLD	RETAIL

selected kentucky galleries

Kentucky Art and Craft Foundation, Louisville

DIRECTIONS
Call for directions.

STUDIO NAME
Dogwood Pottery
STUDIO ADDRESS
3963 Old Newburg Road
Murray, KY   42071
(270) 436-5803

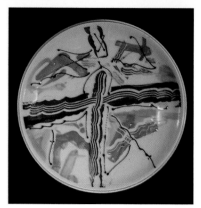

fred shepard

Fred Shepard received his bachelor's degree, master's degree, and master of fine arts degree at Michigan State University, completing his final degree in 1963. He has produced and exhibited his ceramic work throughout the Midwest for more than 35 years. He has been published in a variety of magazines, newspapers, and art journals such as *Craft Horizons* (1966 and 1973), *Ceramics Monthly* (1973), *Art Craft Magazine* (1979), *Studio Potter Magazine* (1987), and the *Louisville Courier Journal* (1996). He is represented in a variety of collections including those belonging to Michigan State University; the Tennessee Arts Commission; the Muse Civico, Bassano Del Grappa, Italy; and the Kentucky Arts Commission. Over his career he has conducted numerous ceramic workshops at places like Sangamon State University in Illinois, Idaho State University, and Dakota State University in South Dakota. Until recently, before his retirement from teaching, he was on the faculty of Murray State University, where he taught from 1963 to 1998, and where he received the Board of Regents Award for Excellence in Teaching in 1998. During this time he also operated his own ceramics studio in Murray called Dogwood Pottery.

Shepard's work is mostly functional stoneware and porcelain vessels fired between 2,000 and 2,400 degrees Fahrenheit. In addition to a full line of functional ware, he also produces various small- and large-scale sculptural forms with surface treatments that go beyond the more traditional glazes one might ordinarily find on utilitarian pieces. His work is fired in a variety of kilns, such as salt and raku. Shepard, a designer and builder of kilns, has constructed over 30 kilns in as many years, all of which have enabled him to pursue his love of creating forms with variable surface effects.

about the artist

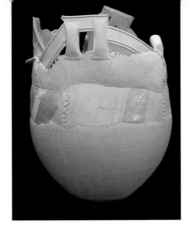

murray

STUDIO HOURS	BY APPOINTMENT
SHOWROOM	YES
HOURS	BY APPOINTMENT
WORK IS SOLD	RETAIL

DIRECTIONS
From Murray, take Hwy. 94 east 8.5 miles. Turn right on Rte. 732. Go 5.2 miles to Old Newburg Road. Turn left onto Old Newburg Road and proceed up the road to the studio.

selected kentucky galleries

Owensboro Museum of Fine Art, Owensboro

STUDIO NAME
The Potter's Touch
STUDIO ADDRESS
2498 Old KY 144
Owensboro, KY   42303
(270) 281-9135
kypotter@aol.com

38

danny dalton

Danny Dalton received a bachelor's degree from Western Kentucky University, where he majored in psychology and minored in art. It was there that he developed a serious interest in pottery. He went on to establish the Potter's Touch in 1987, which he still owns and operates. He sells his work primarily through wholesale/retail shows, as well as some galleries and shops, throughout the United States. He also sells work through a variety of interior design firms and photographic studios, where one-of-a-kind ceramic pieces are used as decorative artworks in furniture advertisements.

Dalton's pottery work is primarily functional stoneware with a wide range of colors and surface treatments. His work often reflects his love for nature through the use of various floral and leaf designs in the glazing process. In addition, he frequently uses leaves, corncobs, and other everyday items to create a wide range of textures on his pieces. Using both throwing techniques and slab construction, he produces teapots, mugs, vases, covered jars, and bowls, along with a range of more decorative pieces, all of which are dishwasher- and microwave-safe. His concern for the utilitarian aspects of his work is certainly apparent, yet the decorative aspects of each piece remain a priority with the work he produces.

Danny

Psalms 16:11

about the artist

owensboro

STUDIO HOURS	8:30 AM-6:30 PM
SHOWROOM	NO
HOURS	N/A
WORK IS SOLD	RETAIL/WHOLESALE

selected kentucky galleries

Marcum's Gallery, Louisville

Artifacts, Bowling Green

DIRECTIONS

From Hwy. 60 (east of Owensboro), take Hwy. 144. Turn right at the three-mile marker onto Jones Road. Take an immediate left onto Old Hwy. 144. The studio is on the right.

STUDIO NAME
Dayman Studio
STUDIO ADDRESS
120 East 24th St.
Owensboro, KY   42303
(270) 926-7313
chrisdayman@aol.com

chris dayman

Chris Dayman received his bachelor of fine arts degree in ceramics from Carnegie-Mellon University in 1972. He went on to complete a master of fine arts degree in ceramics from Ohio State University in 1974. He worked at the Museum of Modern Art in New York City in the late 1970s and was the director of the Crafts Center and Union Gallery at the State University of New York at Stony Brook from 1978 to 1985. He later taught at Concord College in Athens, West Virginia, from 1985 to 1989. Currently he is a professor of art at Owensboro Community College, where he has been on the faculty since 1989.

Dayman has exhibited his ceramic works regularly since 1983 and continues to produce ceramics and drawings for exhibition throughout the region. His work is functional and sculptural, with raku his primary choice of technique in clay. He has always admired works that have a natural, primitive quality, one that is easily obtainable through the raku glazing and firing processes. Through the fire and smoke, as well as the cautious handling of the hot wares, the element of surprise remains an exciting component of his ceramics.

The work of Chris Dayman is powerful in how it often addresses the very nature of conflict within our lives. Many of the works are vertical, monolithic monuments that are referred to as "bounders." Bounders are constructed of sections that are glued together, and their surfaces are often incised with writing and covered with thick, irregular glazes. Other works in clay produced by Dayman are architectural constructions and thrown functional forms, most of which are also raku-fired. Whether it is functional ware or sculptural forms, Dayman's work almost always conveys a sense of purpose.

about the artist

owensboro

STUDIO HOURS	BY APPOINTMENT
SHOWROOM	NO
HOURS	N/A
WORK IS SOLD	RETAIL

selected kentucky galleries

Kentucky Art and Craft Foundation, Louisville

Owensboro Museum of Art, Owensboro

Kentucky Gallery of Fine Art and Craft, Lexington

DIRECTIONS

The studio is on 24th Street, 3 blocks east of Frederica Street (Rte. 431), the main north/south street in Owensboro.

STUDIO NAME
Mulberry Creek Pottery
STUDIO ADDRESS
1206 Locust St.
Owensboro, KY   42301
(270) 683-6803
driver@mindspring.com

steve driver

Stephen Driver received a bachelor's degree in psychology with a minor in constructive design from Florida State University in 1973. In 1974, when he discovered that ceramics would be his career choice, he went to study at the Penland School in North Carolina. In 1975 he accepted an opportunity to work as an apprentice at the Michael Leach Pottery in Devon, England, and then the Coxwold Pottery in York, England, where he studied with British potter, Peter Bruce Dick. After returning to the United States in 1977, he worked in Johnson County, Arizona, as an artist and teacher. It was here that he first opened his production pottery business. During this time he took a break from his business to attend graduate school for two years at the University of Georgia, where he earned a master of fine arts degree in 1988. Driver taught as a visiting professor at the University of the Ozarks[Where is this?] in 1989, the University of Mississippi in 1990, and Southern Arkansas University from 1993 to 1994. He is currently on the faculty of Brescia College in Owensboro, where he has taught since 1994.

Driver's work has been exhibited widely throughout the South and Midwest dating back to 1988. He was a recipient of an Early Times Scholarship in 1999 and an Al Smith Fellowship from the Kentucky Arts Council in 1996, and he has been reviewed in several major ceramics publications.

Stephen Driver's ceramic work is primarily wheel-thrown and functional, yet his concern for form and the development of fresh ideas within the range of utility is what keeps his work innovative. His love for the utilitarian object is present in his forms, but his forms also reflect interests outside of clay, such as poetry, dance, and music. Most of his work is fired in wood or salt kilns. He said, "Some people like to paint on pots. I prefer to paint with the fire." In addition to the more functional pieces in clay, he produces ceramic and bronze sculptures that are concerned with gender and the human condition.

about the artist

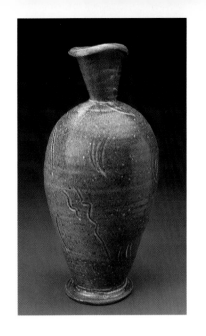

owensboro

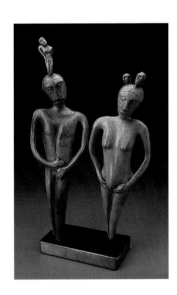

STUDIO HOURS	BY APPOINTMENT
SHOWROOM	NO
HOURS	N/A
WORK IS SOLD	RETAIL

selected kentucky galleries

Kentucky Art and Craft Foundation, Louisville

DIRECTIONS
On Brescia's campus, Lechner Graduate
Center. Frederica and Seventh Street.

STUDIO NAME

STUDIO NAME
Pottery By Thomas
STUDIO ADDRESS
5386 Roby Road
Philpot, KY   42366
(270) 281-5892

thomas r. porter

Thomas Porter was first introduced to ceramics while studying art at Brescia College in Owensboro, where he later completed a bachelor's degree in 1986. He also studied ceramics and art abroad by taking classes in China, Korea, and Japan in 1985 while on a program through the college. He participates in a variety of regional art festivals where he sells his work, and he has pieces in galleries and shops across the United States. He has won several awards for his ceramics through art fairs and exhibitions.

Porter's ceramic work is primarily functional and decorative raku and stoneware. He claims to be influenced by Mediterranean and Oriental styles, with attention to classical forms and colorful surfaces his primary inspiration. In stoneware he produces a range of pieces, such as teapots, vases, bowls, and pitchers, all of which are fired above 2,300 degrees Fahrenheit in reduction and oxidation atmospheres. In raku, his pieces are generally decorative with myriad colorful surfaces on the forms. The development of strong shapes is his first priority, with an attention to surface secondary. He said, "When you have a good form with a good glaze, you have a great piece, but one without the other will only be a good piece." The colorful, variable surface effects on his raku work, combined with the strength of a more traditional shape, help Porter articulate his thoughts about the importance of form and surface and how they work together to create a strong visual effect.

2000

about the artist

philpot

	MONDAY-FRIDAY	SATURDAY
STUDIO HOURS	8 AM-2 PM	8 AM-5 PM
SHOWROOM	YES	
HOURS	MONDAY-FRIDAY	SATURDAY
	8 AM-2 PM	8 AM-5 PM
WORK IS SOLD	RETAIL/WHOLESALE	

selected kentucky galleries

Upstairs Gallery, Berea

The Owensboro Museum of Fine Art, Owensboro

Museum of American Quilter's Society, Paducah

Artique, Lexington

Kentucky Art and Craft Foundation, Louisville

DIRECTIONS

From Owensboro, east on Hwy. 54 to Philpot. Left on Jack Hinton Road. Go approximately 2 miles and turn left on McPherson Road. When the road ends, turn right on Roby Road. Studio is approximately 1/4 mile ahead on right.

STUDIO NAME
Wethington Studio
STUDIO ADDRESS
431 Booth Ave.
Owensboro, KY   42301
(270) 683-2320

cat wethington

Cat Wethington received a bachelor's degree in 1987 from Brescia College in Owensboro and a master of fine arts degree in 1990 from Southern Illinois University in Carbondale. She taught as an adjunct faculty member at Eastern Kentucky University from 1994 to 1997 and at Owensboro Community College in 1999. She has exhibited her work throughout the Midwest dating back to 1985 and has been a visiting artist offering workshops and lectures on her artwork. She sells her work through galleries and exhibitions throughout the region as well as at her own studio.

Wethington's work is mostly coil-built, abstract sculptural vessel forms inspired by nests and water sources. Her stoneware clay creations, fired in salt and reduction kilns, are often elegant studies in form and surface. Careful use of color and glaze, juxtaposed to the rich, textural surface of the clay, helps to create exciting contrasts of surface against form. With an emphasis on "place," the pieces often have horizons and canyons that serve as metaphors for landscapes. The accessibility of interior space often adds a complexity to her forms that challenges the viewer while setting the mood. She said, "What I hope most to express with my work is that the spiritual and the physical are intrinsically, inseparably intertwined and that this dynamic, sensuous, sometimes horrific world is sacred."

about the artist

owensboro

STUDIO HOURS	BY APPOINTMENT
SHOWROOM	NO
HOURS	N/A
WORK IS SOLD	RETAIL

selected kentucky galleries

The Owensboro Museum of Fine Art, Owensboro

DIRECTIONS
Call for directions.

STUDIO NAME
Two Street Studios
STUDIO ADDRESS
409 Broadway
Paducah, KY 42001
(270) 443-2582
sceramic@midwest.net

sarah roush

Sarah Roush received a bachelor of fine arts degree in painting from Northern Kentucky University in 1981 and a master of fine arts degree in printmaking from the University of Cincinnati in 1984. She has exhibited her work regularly dating back to 1982 and currently operates the Two Street Studio in Paducah.

After renovating a 13,000-square-foot vacant department store in downtown Paducah for exhibition and working space, she formed a corporation called Red Ink Ltd., which she serves as president, to restore historic structures.

Roush produces hand-built, low-fire ceramic sculptures. Because of her painting and printmaking background, she regularly uses low-fire glazes in much the same manner that one would paint. Her work is not concerned with utilitarian issues of pottery, and her forms, therefore, often fall between the areas commonly associated with sculpture and painting. Images based on underwater figures and colors allow a variety of metaphors to be explored within her work. Roush said, "There is an undeniable need to extend the painted surface, embody each piece with gesture and presence, to add a dimension, both physical and emotional to my creative image." Her pieces are often attempts to give her two-dimensional paintings a dimensional form, using clay as a canvas.

about the artist

paducah

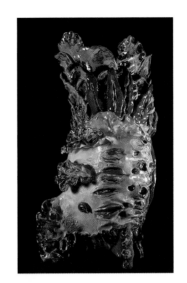

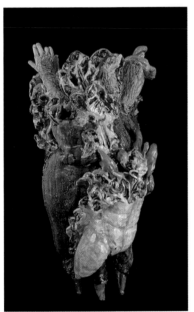

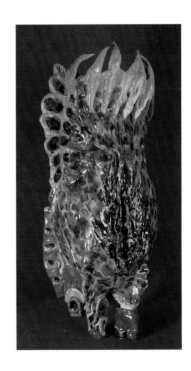

STUDIO HOURS	NONE
SHOWROOM	YES
HOURS	BY APPOINTMENT
WORK IS SOLD	RETAIL/WHOLESALE

selected kentucky galleries

Bowery Gallery, Paducah

Gallery 600, Paducah

DIRECTIONS

Call for directions.

The Bluegrass, synonymous with the famous style of music, is the premier place in the world for breeding of racehorses and the production of famous Kentucky bourbons. The area is known for its limestone strata, which, with the movement of water through the rocks, brings phosphates to the soil, fortifying plants and grass making them perfect food for horses to create strong bones for racing.

bluegrass region

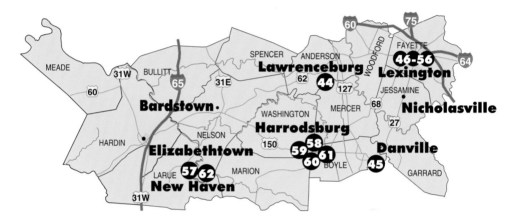

An area of lush, green rolling hills, the Bluegrass is home to several historical places, such as Shaker Village of Pleasant Hill, Old Fort Harrod State Park, and My Old Kentucky Home State Park, to name only a few. Helping to shape this region, the backdrop of academia is ever present. The University of Kentucky, along with the private schools of Centre College, Transylvania University, and Midway College provide ample opportunity for young artists in clay to pursue their careers.

The Bluegrass is also home to Lexington, a cultural hub of the state, where the visual and performing arts thrive amidst a musical variety unique to the area. Clay work is well respected in this region, which is why it is not surprising to see a good amount of ceramists in this book coming from the Bluegrass. The culture of clay in this region is not singular in style or technique, and the wide array of ceramic forms created by artists working here illustrates an awareness of contemporary ceramics linked with a firm understanding of pottery traditions.

Ceramic artists more recently located to the Bluegrass bring a worldly view to the clay scene, while more traditional ceramists continue to demonstrate how continuity in style and location have helped them achieve success in their studio clay work.

STUDIO NAME
Marianne Brown Pottery
STUDIO ADDRESS
2038 Fox Creek Road
Hwy. 62
Lawrenceburg, KY   40342
(502) 859-0602

44

marianne brown

Marianne Brown earned a bachelor of fine arts degree in 1989 from the Memphis College of Art in Memphis, Tennessee. She received further training at the Penland School of Crafts in Penland, North Carolina, and at the Tennessee Technological University in Cookville, Tennessee. Her work has been exhibited regularly in exhibitions and crafts fairs in the region since 1990, and she is a member of the Kentucky Craft Marketing program in Frankfort. She began making her pottery part time over 15 years ago, and for the past three years, she has been operating full time. In addition to running her pottery business, she also teaches classes in ceramics for local residents.

Brown produces a range of utilitarian forms, such as bowls, teapots, vases, cups, and other pieces, that are wheel-thrown and hand-built. The work is oxidation, high-fired in a gas kiln that she built herself at her pottery, and she uses a variety of glazed surfaces meant to enrich the textural areas that are often stamped into her pieces. Ancient stamp designs that she makes herself are pressed into contemporary forms. Interlocking hexagonal designs taken from 13th-century Persian pottery and Mayan and Aztec symbols, along with other patterns from nature, are some of the stamped designs she uses in her work. Brown's fascination with the vessel manifests itself in the creation of handmade, functional pottery forms. She hopes that these provide a "means of expression" within her objects meant for daily use.

Marianne Brown

about the artist

lawrenceburg

STUDIO HOURS	9 AM-5 PM
SHOWROOM	NO
HOURS	N/A
WORK IS SOLD	RETAIL/WHOLESALE

selected kentucky galleries

Artique, Lexington

Capital Gallery, Frankfort

Kentucky Art and Craft Foundation, Louisville

True Kentucky, Glendale

DIRECTIONS

Heading west out of Lawrenceburg on Hwy. 62 (which turns into Fox Creek Road), pass over the Salt River, and the pottery is just past U.S. 513 on the right.

STUDIO NAME
Judith Pointer Studio
STUDIO ADDRESS
Centre College
Danville, KY 40422
(859) 238-5469
pointer@centre.edu

judith pointer

Judith Pointer, born in Las Vegas, Nevada, received an associate degree from Garden City Community College in Holcomb, Kansas, in 1986. She went on to earn a bachelor's degree from the University of Kansas in Lawrence in 1989. She studied ceramics at Southern Illinois University at Edwardsville from 1992 to 1995 and completed a master of fine arts degree in 1998 from the University of Massachusetts at Dartmouth. She was employed as a workshop instructor doing Portuguese tile decoration for the Center for Portuguese Studies at the University of Massachusetts during the summer of 1996 and is currently on the faculty at Centre College in Danville, where she teaches ceramics and drawing. Since graduate school, she has exhibited her work regularly in juried and invitational exhibitions.

Pointer's ceramic work is primarily sculptural in stoneware and porcelain. Oftentimes, she employs mixed media, such as sheetrock, wood, and glass. Her style uses thin clay slabs joined at the edges to form vessels or hollow, sealed objects. Seams are often left exposed to reveal the construction process of the piece. Specifics are pared down, allowing for the essence of a universal form, such as a house, an egg, or a plant. The pieces contain a subtle, sensual beauty in the form and surface of the work, with glazes most often being used to obtain this effect.

danville

STUDIO HOURS	BY APPOINTMENT
SHOWROOM	NO
HOURS	N/A
WORK IS SOLD	RETAIL

DIRECTIONS
Located on the campus of Centre College in Danville, approximately 35 miles south of Lexington. On Beatty Ave. is the Jones Visual Arts Center, where the studio is located.

selected kentucky galleries

Tower Cerlan Gallery, Lexington

STUDIO NAME
Cerlan Art Studio
STUDIO ADDRESS
522 W. Short St.
Lexington, KY   40507
(859) 252-8023
cerlan@aol.com

gayle cerlan

Gayle Cerlan began her art training at the University of Kentucky from 1973 to 1975 and later received a bachelor of fine arts degree from the Louisville School of Art in 1976. She continued her ceramics training at the University of Louisville between 1992 and 1998, where she continues to work toward her master's degree in studio art. She has also taken classes at Alfred University in Alfred, New York, and at the Anderson Ranch School of Art in Colorado.

Cerlan has exhibited her work regularly throughout the region since 1981 and has received grants and/or awards from the Kentucky Crafts Marketing Program, the Kentucky Arts Council, and the Kentucky School for the Blind. Cerlan's work has also been presented in national publications such as *Ceramics Monthly* and *House Beautiful* magazines as well as local newspapers and magazines. She is an active member in the Kentucky ceramics community through her involvement as director of the *Cityworks* exhibition in Louisville (1997), as curator of the national *Dinnerworks* exhibit (1994-7), and as a board member for the Louisville Visual Arts Association (1993-9). She teaches ceramics classes for children and adults and is co-owner of the Tower Cerlan Gallery of Fine Arts in Lexington.

Cerlan's ceramic work is primarily hand-built sculptural forms that are fired in electric kilns. Pieces are generally multifired using the majolica technique in a wide range of colors and with a strong painterly approach to surface. She sometimes uses pit firing to add a smoked layer to the surfaces of the already colorful forms. While pieces can often be viewed as both utilitarian and decorative, her interest in the sculptural juxtaposition of organic shapes with other forms is what makes her work most appealing. Influences in other cultures, architecture, and other craft fields have been personal references for her work in clay. She said, "I like to create works that transcend simple description and extend perception in ways both pleasurable and profoundly personal." Cerlan's ceramic pieces are visually delightful in their use of color and imagery while still challenging the viewer who contemplates the very nature of contemporary ceramic art.

about the artist

lexington

STUDIO HOURS	BY APPOINTMENT
SHOWROOM	NO
HOURS	N/A
WORK IS SOLD	RETAIL

DIRECTIONS

Take the Airport Exit off I-75/I-64 and head toward downtown Lexington. Go approximately 5 miles and turn left onto Main St. Go up to the first traffic light and turn left (Jefferson St.). Go to the next traffic light (one block) and turn right onto Short St. The studio is on the right about 2 blocks on the corner of Short and Felix.

selected kentucky galleries

Tower Cerlan Gallery, Lexington

Kentucky Art and Craft Foundation, Louisville

STUDIO NAME
SDR Pottery
STUDIO ADDRESS
P.O. Box 4594
Lexington, KY   40544
(859) 278-8335
ksdaro@mindspring.com
www.mindspring.com/~ksdaro

steve davis-rosenbaum

about the artist

Steve Davis-Rosenbaum, a native of San Francisco, California, attended Lewis and Clark College in Portland, Oregon, where he received a bachelor's degree in 1978. After moving east in 1980, he worked with ceramists Michael Simon at XXIX Oaks Pottery in Winterville, Georgia, before going on to attend the University of Georgia in Athens, where he completed a master of fine arts degree in 1986. He later found his way to Kentucky, where he became the resident studio potter at Berea College from 1986 to 1988. He has operated the SDR Pottery in Lexington for more than 10 years. Since 1991, he has been an instructor of art at Midway College in Midway, where he shares a position with his wife, Kate, a printmaker.

Davis-Rosenbaum's pottery has been widely exhibited throughout the United States. He has won numerous awards including the Al Smith Fellowship from the Kentucky Arts Council in 1994, the Early Times Scholarship in 1989 and 1997, and other local and regional grants. He has conducted workshops throughout the Midwest and is a frequent consultant on ceramics-related projects. His work has been featured in several major ceramics publications and books such as *The Best of Pottery (I and II),* Angela Fina & Christopher Gustin (Gloucester, Massachusetts: Rockport Publishers, 1996 & 1998 respectively) and *The New Maiolica: Contemporary Approaches to Colour and Techniques* by Mathias Ostermann (University of Pennsylvania Press, Philadelphia, 1999).

SDR Pottery produces a wide range of utilitarian pieces made in the majolica style. All the pieces are handmade from red earthenware clay, coated with a white glaze, and decorated with a variety of colored stains. The pieces are fired in an electric kiln in an oxidation atmosphere to approximately 1,940 degrees Fahrenheit.

Davis-Rosenbaum's distinctive work, rooted in the American studio potter movement, is sold in galleries throughout the state and region. The colorful palette and bold forms are best appreciated when handled by others or presented on the table with food.

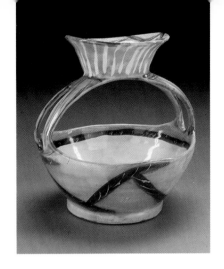

lexington

STUDIO HOURS	BY APPOINTMENT
SHOWROOM	YES
HOURS	BY APPOINTMENT
WORK IS SOLD	RETAIL/WHOLESALE

selected kentucky galleries

Kentucky Art and Craft Foundation, Louisville

Capital Gallery, Frankfort

DIRECTIONS
Call for directions.

STUDIO NAME
Don Glover Designs
STUDIO ADDRESS
2272 Valencia Dr.
Lexington, KY   40513-0907
(859) 224-2444
dgdsgns@aol.com

(48)

don glover

Don Glover received his bachelor's degree in interior design in 1992 from the University of Kentucky, where he was first introduced to ceramics. He has worked as a studio ceramics artist in Lexington from 1993 to the present. He has been a member of the Lexington Art League since 1994 and of the University of Kentucky Fine Arts Institute since 1995, and he is frequently asked by individuals and groups to give private instruction in ceramics . He has enjoyed several exhibitions in galleries across the state and regularly exhibits his work at various juried art shows. Glover sells his work through galleries, wholesale and retail shows, designer shops, and commissions, as well as through his own studio in Lexington.

Glover's ceramic works are primarily wheel-thrown functional and decorative wares. He likes to work with gas-fired salt kilns, oxidation, and raku-fired pottery. He most often creates pieces inspired by classic and organic elements with an emphasis on form and textured surfaces. His work is frequently manipulated after the initial forming process; various hand-built elements are added later. In addition to his functional ware, Glover also produces a series of realistic ceramic fruits and vegetables that are individually hand-thrown, manipulated, textured, and glazed. His work is most known for his interesting, colorful, textured surfaces, which add an exciting visual element to his functional and sculptural work.

about the artist

lexington

STUDIO HOURS	BY APPOINTMENT
SHOWROOM	NO
HOURS	N/A
WORK IS SOLD	RETAIL/WHOLESALE

selected kentucky galleries

Chapman Gallery at Science Hill, Shelbyville

Scarborough Fare, Lexington

Addie Lowe's Lagniappe, Paducah

DIRECTIONS

Studio is located in the Palomar Hills area of Lexington. Drive out of Lexington on Harrodsburg Road and then turn right on Man-o-War Blvd. Turn left at the first light into Palomar Hills sub-division (Lyon Road), and then turn right at the first street. Palomar Blvd. After turning onto Palomar Blvd., turn right onto the first street. Valencia Drive.

STUDIO NAME
Clay Art Designs
STUDIO ADDRESS
1916 Lakes Edge Drive
Lexington, KY   40502
(859) 269-0908
susanraku@aol.com

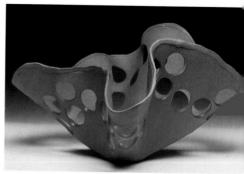

susan goldstein

Susan Goldstein received her bachelor's degree in 1971 from the University of Vermont and then went on to complete a master's degree from Tufts University in Medford, Massachusetts, in 1972. She continued her studies in art through various summer workshops at such noted venues as the Arrowmont School of Arts and Crafts in Gatlinburg, Tennessee; Lake Placid School of Music, Art, and Drama in Lake Placid, New York; and the Parson's School of Design in New York City. She has exhibited her work regularly over the past 10 years and has had her work in several major ceramics publications as well as in the book *Ceramic Design* by Chris Rich (Asheville, N.C.: Lark Books, 2000).

Goldstein has received numerous awards for her ceramics from such notable organizations as the Kentucky Arts Council; the Hoyt Institute of Fine Arts in New Castle, Pennsylvania; and Eastern Washington University in Cheney, Washington. She is also frequently asked to do commissions for various individual and corporate sponsors across the state. In addition, Goldstein has been an active member of the arts community through her involvement with the Lexington Art League, the Kentucky Guild of Artists and Craftsmen (president of the board, 1998-9), the Lexington Arts and Cultural Council, and the Opera House Gallery.

Goldstein's ceramic work, which is both functional and sculptural, is created by waving, undulating, and stretching canvas slabs that take on the uncanny appearance of fabric. With raku her technique of choice, Goldstein's teapots, covered jars, bowls, and delicate wall sculptures define much of her work in ceramics. Clay images vibrate with color that is used to emphasize the textures and the depth of the forms. According to Goldstein, "While my intent is to replicate, my approach deals with growth and motion." Her ceramic fiber pieces often have a gestural quality that gives them a feeling of soft motion in an otherwise rigid finished material.

lexington

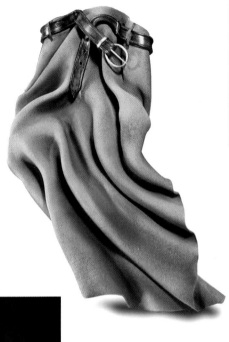

STUDIO HOURS	BY APPOINTMENT
SHOWROOM	YES
HOURS	BY APPOINTMENT
WORK IS SOLD	RETAIL/WHOLESALE

selected kentucky galleries

Kentucky Art and Craft Foundation, Louisville

Images Friedman Gallery, Louisville

DIRECTIONS

Take Moreland Drive off Chinoe, go to the end, and take a right onto Glen Hill. Go straight. Street becomes Lakes Edge Drive. Last house on the right.

STUDIO NAME
Blue Moon Studio Pottery
STUDIO ADDRESS
154 Penmoken Park
Lexington, KY   40503
(859) 278-6916
jlipuma@mindspring.com

janice lipuma

Janice Lipuma received her ceramics education at the University of Kentucky as early as 1975 and again in 1993-4. She has also attended a variety of workshops in the United States, Australia, England, and Canada. She has sold her work at various art shows throughout Kentucky and continues to sell pieces through local shops and galleries.

Lipuma's ceramic work is primarily stoneware tableware as well as vases and teapots that are almost always wheel-thrown. She also does ceramic jewelry boxes that are raku- and sawdust-fired. Her interest is in utilitarian classical forms, which she develops further by using a variety of glazes.

Her love for the functional vessel and how it is used is largely what motivates her to create forms in clay, and she is quick to point out that she sees her role as the "neighborhood potter." She said, "I expect my pots to look elegant, feel good in the hands, and work right. The lucky pot boasts a small kiss from the kiln gods. Good pots, like people, travel a long history of becoming." Her simple, utilitarian pieces often make this conversion from the common to something special, in particular with how they find their place within the life of the user.

Lipuma

about the artist

lexington

STUDIO HOURS	8 AM-4:30 PM
SHOWROOM	YES
HOURS	BY APPOINTMENT
WORK IS SOLD	RETAIL/WHOLESALE

selected kentucky galleries

Completely Kentucky, Frankfort

Moby Maple, Lexington

DIRECTIONS

Penmoken Park is just south of Central Baptist Hospital off Nicholasville Road.

STUDIO NAME
Woodland Park Pottery
STUDIO ADDRESS
188 Woodland Ave., #2
Lexington, KY 40502
(859) 233-0085
artmolin@acs.eku.edu
www.uky.edu/
Artsource/molinaro

51

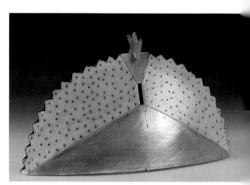

joe molinaro

Joe Molinaro received a bachelor's degree in 1975 from Ball State University in Muncie, Indiana. He completed a master of fine art degree in 1978 from Southern Illinois University in Carbondale. He has exhibited his work regularly in the United States and abroad dating back to 1977 and has won numerous awards, among them the Rude Osolnik Award in 2000 from the Kentucky Art and Craft Foundation and the Kentucky Craft Marketing Program, an Al Smith Fellowship from the Kentucky Arts Council in 1996, an Early Times Scholarship in 1999, and a Fulbright Research Award (Ecuador) in 1994. He is frequently invited to conduct workshops and give lectures on his work in clay and on his research into the pottery traditions of the Upper Amazon basin region of Ecuador. His work is represented in a variety of collections and has been reviewed in a number of prestigious publications. He is also the author of numerous articles on ceramics and has produced a video documentary on the Quichua Indian potters of the Amazon. In addition, he founded the Clayart Listserv in 1994, an electronic discussion group with more than 2,500 members from over 30 countries dedicated to the advancement of ceramics via the Internet. His work can be seen in several galleries in the region, and he currently teaches in the art department at Eastern Kentucky University in Richmond.

Molinaro's ceramic work is primarily sculptural porcelain vessels fired to above 2,300 degrees Fahrenheit in oxidation and reduction atmospheres. He also produces a line of more utilitarian wares in porcelain and stoneware. Some of his work, which is both functional and sculptural, is fired in wood- and salt-fired kilns.

His pottery has always maintained a focus on utilitarian forms and how they find their place within a contemporary society. Glazes are often used to provide a tactile and visually diverse surface, while volumetric forms offer a sculptural base from which to explore tradition. Whether he produces sculptural vessels or elegant serving dishes for the table, Molinaro's concern with the role of pottery in our lives remains constant in his work.

about the artist

lexington

STUDIO HOURS	BY APPOINTMENT
SHOWROOM	NO
HOURS	N/A
WORK IS SOLD	RETAIL/WHOLESALE

selected kentucky galleries

Kentucky Art and Craft Foundation, Louisville

Images Friedman Gallery, Louisville

Tower Cerlan Gallery, Lexington

DIRECTIONS

Heading east on Main St. from downtown Lexington, turn right onto Woodland Ave. Go 2 blocks until you are at the intersection of Woodland Ave. and High St. The studio is on the second floor of the large brick building on your left located at the intersection.

STUDIO NAME
Wyman Rice Studio
STUDIO ADDRESS
379 Virginia Ave.
Lexington, KY
40502
(859) 266-8451

wyman rice

Wyman Rice [signature]

Wyman Rice studied ceramics and English at the University of Kentucky in the 1970s and 1980s. He has steadily produced work in the Central Kentucky area for nearly 20 years and operates the Wyman Rice Studio in Lexington. He has taught at a number of venues, such as the Open Ground Art Camp in Harrodsburg in 1997 and 1998; the Lexington Art League in 1995; Asbury College in Wilmore in 1994; and the Great Montana Clay Getaway in Roscoe, Montana, in 1992 and 1993. He has exhibited his ceramic work regularly dating back to 1985 and has received numerous awards, including a Merit Award from Arts Fest in Santa Rosa Beach, Florida; a Purchase Award from the Woodland Art Fair in 1998; a First Place Award in ceramics from the Cherokee Art Fair in Louisville in 1995; and a Best of Show Award from the Kentucky Guild of Artists and Craftsmen's Spring Fair in 1991. His work is sold in various galleries throughout the state and region.

Rice's ceramic work is hand-built using mostly slab and coils and is fired in either raku or electric kilns. He is concerned most with sculptural forms and less with how pieces function. While there may be a suggestion of utility in some of his pieces, he says that the real focus of his work is the sculptural side. Rice said, "As a visual artist, my work is primarily about form, with little or no thought to function, although function may be implied or suggested by form." His pieces are often strong, volumetric forms, some with sharp edges to help define the shape. Some larger coil-built forms have a figurative reference while maintaining potlike qualities. Glazes and stains used with the raku process add to the overall surface characteristics of the form. Other pieces are fired in electric kilns and have a simple, unglazed surface emphasizing the material itself.

lexington

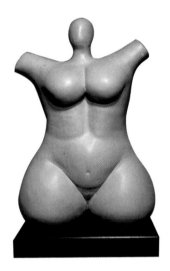

STUDIO HOURS	11 AM-5:30 PM or BY APPOINTMENT
SHOWROOM	NO
HOURS	N/A
WORK IS SOLD	RETAIL/WHOLESALE

selected kentucky galleries

Kentucky Gallery of Fine Craft and Art, Lexington

Kentucky Art and Craft Foundation, Louisville

Edenside Gallery, Louisville

Completely Kentucky, Frankfort

Raintree Gallery, Versailles

Bebe's Artisan Market, Paducah

DIRECTIONS
From Main St., south on Broadway to Virginia Ave., left on Virginia Ave.

STUDIO NAME
Selter
STUDIO ADDRESS
665 Longview Drive
Lexington, KY   40503
(859) 278-7168
dselter@mail.transy.edu

dan selter

Dan Selter began his art training at the Louisville School of Art, where he received a bachelor of fine arts degree in 1973. He went on to Syracuse University where he completed a master of fine arts degree in 1975. He has exhibited his ceramic artwork dating back to 1977 and has received a number of awards, including a Special Friend of Families Award from the Lexington Family Care Center and the Bingham Award for Excellence in Teaching from Transylvania University, where he is currently a faculty member. His work is represented in numerous collections in the state, such as those of the Brown-Forman Corp., the Rev. and Mrs. Shands, Kentucky Fried Chicken Inc., all in Louisville; and the Farmer's National Bank in Lebanon. His work is also sold in various galleries throughout the state.

Selter's ceramic works are mostly sculptural stoneware vessels that are usually figurative and hand-built and often fired in soda-vapor kilns to temperatures above 2,000 degrees Fahrenheit. Whether he works entirely with a figurative reference or makes pots for use, the work is often playful and colorful, giving it a visually exciting life all its own. He claims that the appeal to make ceramic objects is that the process is timeless and ubiquitous. Selter said, "Some pots made today look much like pots made 10,000 years ago. Clay pots are the closest thing we have to a cultural common denominator. . . . It's possible that the aesthetic availability of ceramic objects is the only thing keeping this archaic craft alive in this technological age." His work often provides a narrative and offers the viewer a special look, while still finding ways to function in the viewer's life.

about the artist

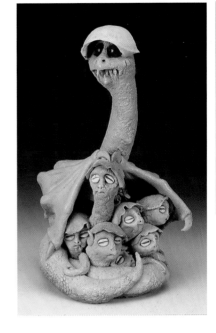

lexington

STUDIO HOURS	BY APPOINTMENT
SHOWROOM	NO
HOURS	N/A
WORK IS SOLD	RETAIL

selected kentucky galleries

Kentucky Gallery of Fine Crafts and Art, Lexington

Kentucky Art and Craft Foundation, Louisville

Water Tower Gallery, Louisville

DIRECTIONS
Call for directions.

54 STUDIO NAME
Kate Sprengnether
STUDIO ADDRESS
606 N. Broadway, #2
Lexington, KY   40508
(859) 225-4906

kate sprengnether

Kate Sprengnether studied art at the University of Dayton from 1987 to 1990 and went on to receive a bachelor's degree at Ursuline College in Cleveland, Ohio, in 1993. She later earned a master of fine arts degree in ceramics from Syracuse University in Syracuse, New York, in 1996. She has exhibited her artwork steadily since 1992 and has received several awards. She regularly participates in a host of professional activities including the College Art Association's (CAA) annual conference, the National Council for the Education of the Ceramic Arts (NCECA), and many workshops and lectures. Sprengnether has been a resident artist at Hartwick College in Oneonta, New York; an adjunct faculty member at the State University of New York in Oneonta; a visiting professor at Weslyan College in Macon, Georgia; and an adjunct faculty member in ceramics at the University of Kentucky.

Sprengnether's ceramic pieces are hand-built sculptural forms most often inspired by natural objects such as seashells, seed pods and nests. Made mostly of earthenware clays, her pieces often exhibit rich textural surfaces decorated with layers of underglaze colors and carving. Bold forms allow for detailed surface explorations that enhance the metaphor, both of which keep the work visually and intellectually appealing. Sprengnether said, "I hope to make work that reminds the viewer of a natural object, while at the same time forcing them to recognize the hand of the maker and to realize that this piece is man-made."

about the artist

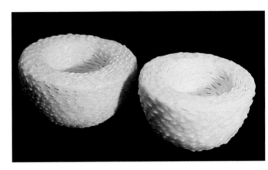
lexington

STUDIO HOURS	BY APPOINTMENT
SHOWROOM	NO
HOURS	N/A
WORK IS SOLD	RETAIL

selected kentucky galleries

Tower Cerlan Gallery, Lexington

DIRECTIONS
Call for directions.

STUDIO NAME
Woodland Park Studio
STUDIO ADDRESS
188 Woodland Ave., #2
Lexington, KY 40502
(859) 254-5612
lsprulock@jessamine.
k12.ky.us

liz spurlock

Spurlock

Liz Spurlock received a bachelor's degree in education and a bachelor of fine arts degree from Eastern Kentucky University in 1993. She later went on to Edinboro University in Pennsylvania, where she completed her master of fine arts degree in 1996. She has exhibited her work in Kentucky, Pennsylvania, Indiana, and Illinois, dating back to 1991 and has been the recipient of several awards, including an Early Times Scholarship in 1998 and a Friends of Arrowmont Scholarship in 1992. She taught part time at the Erie Art Museum in 1995, at Eastern Kentucky University in 1996, and at the Headley-Whitney Museum in Lexington in 1998. She sells her work through several galleries and shops in the region and maintains a studio in Lexington.

Spurlock's ceramic work is primarily wheel-thrown and altered functional ware. She produces a wide range of utilitarian pieces, mostly teapots, serving trays, cups, and bowls. Using minimal glazes, she prefers to fire in atmospheric kilns such as wood, salt and/or soda. These firings create a soft, visual effect on the surface of her forms that makes one want to touch and hold them, emphasizing her love for pots that are meant to be handled and used every day. Her style is forms with a gestural quality, often with bold surface marks made while the clay is still soft. This human touch on the pieces allows the action of ash and flame to cover her forms and to create patterns that speak of material and process. Spurlock said, "A celebration of form and function encourages my vessels to be handled and used for the serving of food, which, in turn, nourishes and sustains us." Spurlock's work is a true culmination of idea and intent, with the finished product often an example of a pot with an attitude.

about the artist

lexington

STUDIO HOURS	BY APPOINTMENT
SHOWROOM	NO
HOURS	N/A
WORK IS SOLD	RETAIL/WHOLESALE

selected kentucky galleries

Kentucky Art and Craft Foundation, Louisville

Images Friedman Gallery, Louisville

DIRECTIONS

Heading east on Main St. from downtown Lexington, turn right onto Woodland Ave. Go 2 blocks until you are at the intersection of Woodland Ave. and High St. The studio is on the second floor of the large brick building on your left located at the intersection.

STUDIO NAME
Stofer Fine Arts
STUDIO ADDRESS
401 W. Main Street, Suite 112
Victorian Square
Lexington, KY   40506
(859) 258-9863

jill coldiron stofer

Jill Coldiron Stofer received her bachelor's degree from the University of Kentucky in 1984 and has been exhibiting her ceramic work in the region dating back to 1986. She has been an adjunct instructor of ceramics in the College of Fine Arts at the University of Kentucky since 1994 and has taught private studio art lessons at the Artists' Attic Studios in Lexington since 1991. She has been involved in the Lexington community for over 15 years as a ceramic artist and educator and maintains a private studio at Victorian Square in downtown Lexington. She sells her work by private commission through local galleries and shops and at her own studio.

Stofer's ceramic work consists mostly of functional pottery, with a small portion of work in the form of decorative clay murals and sculptural pieces, some of which are raku-fired. Utilitarian forms (cups, teapots, pitchers, bowls, etc.) and how these pieces are used in the home are her primary concern in clay. Work fired in electric and gas kilns, some salt-fired, makes up the bulk of her work, which is meant for daily use.

Some of her sculptural pieces are low-fired with underglazes on red earthenware clay. Areas of the forms are left unglazed where textures have been imprinted into the clay while still wet. Stofer said, "As an artist I simply have a need to create objects and explore the different surface possibilities." Work with a painterly look through color juxtaposition and surface manipulation allows these pieces to exist on many levels beyond traditional clay work.

about the artist

Jill Coldiron

lexington

STUDIO HOURS	BY APPOINTMENT
SHOWROOM	YES
HOURS	BY APPOINTMENT
WORK IS SOLD	RETAIL

DIRECTIONS

Victorian Square is located on the corner of Main St. and Broadway in Lexington. Take exit 113 off of I-75 and follow Broadway about six miles into downtown Lexington.

selected kentucky galleries

Main Cross Gallery, Lexington

57

STUDIO NAME
Fox Hollow Pottery
STUDIO ADDRESS
2795 Younger's
Creek Road
New Haven, KY   40051
(270) 549-8225
foxpots@bardstown.com

jean cochran

Jean Cochran operates the Fox Hollow Pottery in New Haven and is primarily a self-taught potter who received additional training at St. John's Community College in Palatka, Florida. She also took private lessons and attended a variety of ceramics workshops, where she has had the opportunity to work alongside such noted artists as Byron Temple and Paula Winokur. She has conducted a variety of workshops throughout the state, has served as an artist-in-residence through the Kentucky Arts Council, and has taught at various schools throughout the state. She exhibits her work often and participates in a variety of prestigious retail, juried art shows. Her work is sold in a variety of art galleries in and around Kentucky.

Cochran's work is primarily hand-formed on the potter's wheel and is meant to be used. Functional forms such as punch bowls, ladles, cups, and mugs, as well as plates, platters, teapots, and vases, make up her line of utilitarian forms. Intensive hues of blue, teal, iron reds, and black make up her palette, all high-fired in one of her two reduction kilns and sold through art fairs, galleries, or her own showroom, which is located in a 150-year-old log cabin. While her forming and glazing techniques are simple, the result is a body of work that exhibits quiet elegance through design and technique.

Jean Cochran, working with two assistants, maintains a steady output of pottery forms that makes up the line of wares produced at Fox Hollow Pottery.

about the artist

new haven

STUDIO HOURS	BY APPOINTMENT
SHOWROOM	YES
HOURS	BY APPOINTMENT
WORK IS SOLD	RETAIL/WHOLESALE

selected kentucky galleries

Louisville Visual Arts Association, Louisville

Various Kentucky State Park Gift Shops

The Kentucky Horse Park, Lexington

Dinner Bell Restaurant's Gift Shop, Berea

Kentucky Art and Craft Foundation, Louisville

Upstairs Gallery, Berea

DIRECTIONS

From Elizabethtown, take the Bluegrass Parkway (exit 93 off I-65). Exit toward Lyon's Station at exit 8 (Younger's Creek/Lyon's Station Exit). Turn right at the mailbox with the Fox Hollow sign/logo and proceed down a gravel road about 1,000 feet to the studio.

STUDIO NAME
Crosswinds Pottery
STUDIO ADDRESS
340 Henry Robinson Road
Harrodsburg, KY   40330
(859) 366-4439
crosswindspottery@yahoo.com

58

cynthia carr

Cynthia Carr began her ceramics training in the early 1970s at the Pewabic Pottery and Wayne State University, both in Michigan. She received her bachelor of fine arts degree in 1973 from the Cleveland Institute of Art in Ohio, followed by a master of fine arts degree in ceramics from Tulane University in New Orleans, Louisiana, in 1975. In addition to running Crosswinds Pottery, she served as an artist-in-residence and as an active member of the Kentucky Guild of Artists and Craftsmen. She has won several awards for her ceramics and sells pieces in many galleries throughout the state and region.

Carr, founder and owner of Crosswinds Pottery, produces a line of wheel-thrown and handmade pottery. Simple forms finished with high-temperature reduction glazes and fired in a homemade gas kiln define the product line produced at Crosswinds Pottery.

The work, while simple in design, carries with it a strong sense of utility and beauty. Earth tones complement the sturdy forms and reflect the rural and simple lifestyle of the potter. The process, like the finished product, is straightforward; all aspects of her pottery are done by hand, from the mixing of the clay and glaze materials to the firing of the wares.

Each piece is individually handmade, but as part of the potter's line of wares, is consistent from one firing to the next. The lead-free glazes applied to the forms allow for easy use in the home and are dishwasher-, oven-, and microwave-safe.

about the artist

harrodsburg

STUDIO HOURS	BY APPOINTMENT
SHOWROOM	YES
HOURS	BY APPOINTMENT
WORK IS SOLD	RETAIL/WHOLESALE

selected kentucky galleries

Kentucky Art and Craft Foundation, Louisville

Appalachian Fireside Gallery, Berea

Artique, Lexington

Shaker Village of Pleasant Hill, Harrodsburg

A Niche in Thyme, Harrodsburg

Various State Park Gift Shops

Bebe's Artisan Market, Paducah

DIRECTIONS

Follow Hwy. 127 north from Harrodsburg to Hwy. 1160/Talmage-Mayo Road or Hwy. 1988/Vanarsdall Road. Go west 10 miles. Henry Robinson Road is on the right and past the Mt. Hebron Methodist Church and Cemetery.

59

STUDIO NAME
Frasca-Strecker Studio
STUDIO ADDRESS
413 Coghill Lane
Harrodsburg, KY   40330
(859) 734-5271
mafrasca@hotmail.com

michael a. frasca

Michael Frasca studied art at the Cincinnati Art Academy from 1968 to 1972, where he had an emphasis in ceramics, sculpture, and photography. He later was the recipient of a scholarship through the Art Academy and was able to travel abroad for continued study in 1972. He has conducted various teaching workshops in Kentucky and Ohio and has had numerous commissions doing indoor and outdoor sculptures in clay. He has also received several awards for his ceramics including Kentucky Arts Council's Al Smith Fellowship in 2000. He worked as an adjunct faculty member at Northern Kentucky University from 1990 to 1994, where he taught courses in throwing for intermediate students, beginning ceramics, and kiln building. In addition, he was founder of the Spring Street Pottery in Cincinnati (1978-97), where he produced a line of functional and sculptural work that he sold to galleries across the United States. He currently sells his work at the Frasca-Strecker Studio in Harrodsburg, at various retail art fairs in the region, and as individual commissioned pieces.

Frasca's pottery is now primarily functional wheel-thrown stoneware that is single-fired using wood ash glazes. Clean, utilitarian forms with beautiful surface treatments are the cornerstone of his production. His interest in how form and glaze come together is apparent in his functional pieces, all of which make quiet, elegant statements about the beauty of pottery. This pottery is primarily meant for use within the home. After 18 years of producing pieces using wood ash glazes, he has obtained the necessary skills to create well-thrown forms that have a sophisticated look through form and surface. His pottery most often shows his love for creating utilitarian pieces that work as both functional pieces and as visual statements of beauty.

about the artist

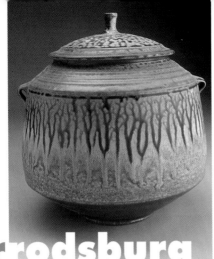

selected works

harrodsburg

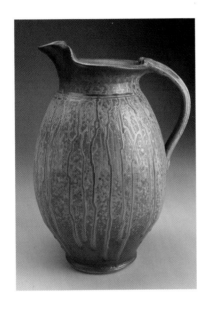

STUDIO HOURS	BY APPOINTMENT
SHOWROOM	YES
HOURS	BY APPOINTMENT
WORK IS SOLD	RETAIL

selected kentucky galleries

Harrodsburg General Store, Harrodsburg

DIRECTIONS

Two miles east from Shakertown off Hwy. 68, a short lane called Coghill.

STUDIO NAME
Peace Roots Pottery
STUDIO ADDRESS
366 Coghill Lane
Harrodsburg, KY
40330
(859) 734-5271

chris strecker

Chris Strecker has been a full-time studio potter for over 30 years, having studied at the Arrowmont School of Arts and Crafts in Gatlinburg, Tennessee; Wooster College in Wooster, Ohio; and the Penland School of Crafts in Penland, North Carolina. She is an active member of the Kentucky Crafts Marketing Program and the Kentucky Guild of Artists and Craftsmen.

Strecker sells her work regularly throughout the region and most often through her Peace Roots Pottery studio in Harrodsburg. She is best known for her line of high-fired stoneware pottery, frequently with copper red glazes, fired in gas kilns. Utilitarian wares such as pitchers, bowls, cups, and saucers are only part of the wide variety of forms found in her pottery, all of which are meant to serve the needs of daily living for eating and drinking. Strecker finds her love and strength in working with clay in pottery meant for everyday use, which is evident in the forms she creates. She said, "It has been my privilege to have made my way in life in clay. I have made pots for many years and can't imagine doing anything else." Though her life is a testimony to her endurance in the field of craft, she continues to maintain an excitement in working with tradition.

about the artist

Chris Strecker

PEACE ROOTS
STUDIO

harrodsburg

STUDIO HOURS	BY APPOINTMENT
SHOWROOM	YES
HOURS	BY APPOINTMENT
WORK IS SOLD	RETAIL

DIRECTIONS
Three miles northeast of Shakertown off Hwy. 68 (outside of Harrodsburg), Coghill Lane is on the left. Studio is on Peace Roots Farm, about 3/4 mile down the lane.

selected kentucky galleries

Harrodsburg General Store, Harrodsburg

STUDIO NAME
Frasca-Strecker Studio
STUDIO ADDRESS
413 Coghill Lane
Harrodsburg, KY   40330
(859) 734-5271
zoeayn@hotmail.com

zoé ayn strecker

Zoé Ayn Strecker received her bachelor's degree in English literature at Grinnell College, Grinnell, Iowa, in 1988, and in 1987, spent one year in Athens, Greece, studying classical sculpture and modern language. She completed a master of fine arts degree in sculpture in 1997 at New York State College of Ceramics at Alfred University in New York. She has exhibited her artwork throughout the region since 1987 and has received several awards, including an Al Smith Fellowship from the Kentucky Arts Council in 1998, a Thayer Fellowship from the State University of New York in 1997, and an Arts/Industry Work Residency from the Louisville Firebrick Co. at Olive Hill. She is also the author of *Kentucky off the Beaten Path: A Guide to Unique Places* (Old Saybrook, Conn.: Globe Pequot Press, 1992).

Strecker's ceramic work is primarily sculptural and architectural. Pieces are generally hand formed by the artist either by direct sculpting techniques or by making molds from sculpted forms and then altering each piece. It is her goal to create large sculptural pieces that afford the viewer the opportunity to pay more attention to all means of physical communication. Strecker said, "My hope is that, in response, perceivers are encouraged to pay heightened attention to all means of physical communication — tactile, visual, olfactory, aural — how these sophisticated tools link up with imagination and intellect to make us fully human." Strecker's ceramic sculptures are most often environments, much like architecture in how it often commands personal, physical space. Work that requires effort is part of what makes her ceramic works unique.

about the artist

harrodsburg

STUDIO HOURS	BY APPOINTMENT
SHOWROOM	YES
HOURS	BY APPOINTMENT
WORK IS SOLD	RETAIL

DIRECTIONS
Three miles northeast of Shakertown off
Hwy. 68 (outside of Harrodsburg), Coghill
Lane is on the left. Studio is on Peace
Roots Farm, about 3/4 mile down the lane

selected kentucky galleries

Kentucky Art and Craft Foundation, Louisville

STUDIO NAME
Lee Pottery
STUDIO ADDRESS
2266 Monks Road
New Haven, KY   40051
(502) 549-3964

62

michael zoeller

Michael Zoeller received a bachelor's degree in economics from Bellarmine College in 1968. He earned a bachelor of fine arts degree in ceramics in 1973 from the Louisville School of Art and a master of fine arts degree from the University of Kansas in 1975. He has taught at a number of venues, such as the University of Kansas, as well as at local adult education and summer camps in the Louisville area.

Zoeller's work has been exhibited throughout the United States in a number of juried and invitational exhibitions, and he regularly sells his work in the region through galleries and commissions. He has worked for over 20 years making pottery in a rural setting south of Louisville.

Zoeller's ceramic works are a combination of wheel-thrown utilitarian ware and occasional sculptural work. He enjoys producing functional pieces that people can use and understand and that therefore easily find a place in their daily lives. His primary line of production ware is stoneware high-fired in kilns that he has built himself. Zoeller said, "I am fairly satisfied making functional pottery that many people can understand, use, and afford. . . . I work alone, but I don't feel lonely." His bold, utilitarian forms, which all have surfaces that reflect the very nature of clay and glaze, help define his line of pottery meant for daily use.

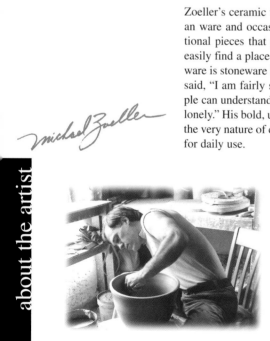

about the artist

new haven

STUDIO HOURS	BY APPOINTMENT
SHOWROOM	NO
HOURS	N/A
WORK IS SOLD	RETAIL/WHOLESALE

selected kentucky galleries

Completely Kentucky, Frankfort

Bardstown Booksellers, Bardstown

Appalachian Fireside Crafts, Berea

Southernland Gallery, Bardstown

Harrodsburg Pottery, Harrodsburg

DIRECTIONS
Call for directions.

Joe Molinaro received a bachelor's degree from Ball State University in 1975 and a Master of Fine Arts in ceramics from Southern Illinois University/Carbondale in 1977. He taught at Broward Community College in Ft. Lauderdale, Florida, from 1981 to 1989 and is currently a professor of art at Eastern Kentucky University, where he is also area chair of the ceramics program (http://www.art.eku.edu/MOLINARO/). Molinaro has been the recipient of two Fulbright Awards in

joe molinaro

Joe in Sig-Sig, Ecuador, 1999

Ecuador (1994 and 2000), where he has been studying the pottery of the upper Amazon basin region for more than 10 years. He has produced a video documentary on the Quichua Indian potters of this region, written articles for various international ceramic magazines, and taught at the Universidad del Azuay in Cuenca, Ecuador. He is currently working on his second video documentary, which portrays the women potters of Jatumpamba, a remote pottery village in the mountains of southern Ecuador. He has twice worked in Ecuador as a consultant for the United States Information Service, first as a cultural specialist, second as an educational specialist. Molinaro's particular interest in traditional pottery south of the U.S. border has brought him in contact with potters from various locations throughout Latin America and the Caribbean. He has documented and written about potters from Jamaica, Mexico, and Guatemala and, more recently, has remained focused on the pottery-making traditions in Ecuador and the upper Amazon basin. In addition, he continues to lead groups of artists on field trips to various Latin American countries to study pottery and craft traditions. Joe Molinaro is also the founder and past moderator of the Clayart list (an electronic e-mail listserv serving thousands of ceramic artists worldwide) as well as co-organizer of the popular Virtual Ceramics Exhibit (the first international ceramics competition held entirely on the Internet (http://www.ilpi.com/artsource/vce/welcome.html). Molinaro has been the recipient of numerous grants and awards, such as the prestigious 2000 Rude Osolnik Award, presented by the Kentucky Craft Marketing Program and the Kentucky Art and Craft Foundation, for his contributions to the field of craft; a Kentucky Arts Council Al Smith Artist's Fellowship; the Moretti Award of South Florida for Artistic Achievement; and a Florida Arts Council Artist's Fellowship. In addition to jurying shows and curating exhibitions, he remains active here and abroad by regularly conducting workshops and giving lectures on a variety of ceramics-related topics. He continues to produce new work in clay and has participated in over 125 solo and group exhibitions over the past 20 years. Along with his teaching, writing, and travels, Molinaro maintains a studio in Lexington, where he lives with his wife, Mary.

Anagama   A type of kiln fired with wood and built on a slope of ground, typically creating interesting visual results from the ash deposited on the wares.

Burnish   A smooth, shiny surface on clay created by rubbing the surface while wet.

Coil-built   A technique for creating clay forms using rope-like pieces of clay.

Cones   Objects used to measure the temperature in the kiln.

glossary of terms

Earthenware   Low-temperature clay, generally red or tan in color.

Electric kiln   A furnace (kiln) that uses electricity as the vehicle for heat distribution.

Engobe   A liquid clay slip colored with stains or oxides and applied over the form for decoration.

Fire/Firing   The heating of ceramic objects.

Gas kiln   A furnace (kiln) that uses gas to create heat.

Glaze   A glass-like surface on clay.

Handbuilt   Creating clay forms without the use of a potter's wheel, using techniques such as coiling, slab, and pinch.

Kiln   A furnace used for firing ceramic objects.

Majolica (Maiolica)   Earthenware covered with a white glaze and colored stains.

Oxidation   A firing with the kiln atmosphere having sufficient oxygen.

Pit-firing   The primitive firing of clay objects without the use of a kiln.

Porcelain   A hard, nonporous, white clay fired to high temperatures.

Potter's wheel   A forming tool used to shape clay objects.

Raku   A Japanese firing process, with or without glaze, where the pieces are pulled out of the hot fire for particular surface effects.

Reduction   A firing with the kiln atmosphere not having sufficient oxygen.

Pinch   Shaping a clay form with the fingers by pinching.

Salt-firing   A glazed surface created by throwing salt into a hot kiln.

Saggar   A semi-closed clay container used to fire ware within a kiln.

Sgraffito   Scratching through one colored surface to reveal the clay color below.

Slab   A flat piece of clay from which forms are made.

Slip   A suspension of clay in water to create a creamy consistency.

Slip cast   Creating forms using plaster molds and liquid clay slip.

Stoneware   A high-temperature clay with little or no absorbency.

Thrown   An object made on the potter's wheel.

Wood-firing   Firing a kiln using wood as the fuel.

artist index

ARTIST	PAGE
Andre, Yerger	12
Austin, Lisa	14
Bates, Wayne	82
Brown, Marianne	102
Carr, Cynthia	130
Cerlan, Gayle	106
Choo, Fong	16
Coakes, Michelle	18
Cochran, Jean	128
Cole, Teresa	54
Culbreth, Sarah	56
Dalton, Danny	88
Davis-Rosenbaum, Steve	108
Dayman, Chris	90
Driver, Steve	92
Elswick, Amy,	20
Enge, Jeff	56
England, Ana	40
Ferguson, Wayne	22
Frasca, Michael	132
Frederick, Sarah	24
Glover, Don	110
Goldstein, Susan	112
Heffner, Gwen	58
Hyleck, Walter	60
Kruer, Diane	44
Leake, Peggy	26
LeGris, Ann	46
Lipuma, Janice	114
Marsh, Ginny	28
Martin, John	62
McClorey, Meg	74
Miner, Judy	30
Molinaro, Joe	116
O'Brian, Susan	84
Oliver, Colette	42
Pointer, Judith	104
Porter, Thomas	94
Reitz, Tom	68
Reneau, Davie	72
Rice, Wyman	118
Rickman, Mitchell	76
Ripley, Trent	64
Ross, Laura	32
Rounsavall, Mary	34
Roush, Sarah	98
Rowe, Melvin	36
Seigel, Greg	48
Selter, Dan	120
Shepard, Fred	86
Smith, Malcolm Mobutu	78
Sprengnether, Kate	122
Spurlock, Liz	124
Stofer, Jill Coldiron	126
Strecker, Chris	134
Strecker, Zoe	136
Temple, Byron	38
Ware, Michael	52
Watson, Larry	10
Wethington, Cat	96
Wright, James	66
Zoeller, Michael	138

by region

REGION	ARTIST	PAGE
Bluegrass	Brown, Marianne	102
Bluegrass	Carr, Cynthia	130
Bluegrass	Cerlan, Gayle	106
Bluegrass	Cochran, Jean	128
Bluegrass	Davis-Rosenbaum, Steve	108
Bluegrass	Frasca, Michael	132
Bluegrass	Glover, Don	110
Bluegrass	Goldstein, Susan	112
Bluegrass	Lipuma, Janice	114
Bluegrass	Molinaro, Joe	116
Bluegrass	Pointer, Judith	104
Bluegrass	Rice, Wyman	118
Bluegrass	Selter, Dan	120
Bluegrass	Sprengnether, Kate	122
Bluegrass	Spurlock, Liz	124
Bluegrass	Stofer, Jill Coldiron	126
Bluegrass	Strecker, Chris	134
Bluegrass	Strecker, Zoe	136
Bluegrass	Zoeller, Michael	138
Cumberland	McClorey, Meg	74
Cumberland	Reneau, Davie	72
Cumberland	Rickman, Mitchell	76
Cumberland	Smith, Malcolm Mobutu	78
Highlands	Cole, Teresa	54
Highlands	Culbreth, Sarah	56
Highlands	Enge, Jeff	56
Highlands	Heffner, Gwen	58
Highlands	Hyleck, Walter	60
Highlands	Martin, John	62
Highlands	Reitz, Tom	68
Highlands	Ripley, Trent	64
Highlands	Ware, Michael	52
Highlands	Wright, James	66
Lakes	Bates, Wayne	82
Lakes	Dalton, Danny	88
Lakes	Dayman, Chris	90
Lakes	Driver, Steve	92
Lakes	O'Brian, Susan	84
Lakes	Porter, Thomas	94
Lakes	Roush, Sarah	98
Lakes	Shepard, Fred	86
Lakes	Wethington, Cat	96
River	Andre, Yerger	12
River	Austin, Lisa	14
River	Choo, Fong	16
River	Coakes, Michelle	18
River	Elswick, Amy,	20
River	England, Ana	40
River	Ferguson, Wayne	22
River	Frederick, Sarah	24
River	Kruer, Diane	44
River	Leake, Peggy	26
River	LeGris, Ann	46
River	Marsh, Ginny	28
River	Miner, Judy	30
River	Oliver, Colette	42
River	Ross, Laura	32
River	Rounsavall, Mary	34
River	Rowe, Melvin	36
River	Seigel, Greg	48
River	Temple, Byron	38
River	Watson, Larry	10

by county

COUNTY	ARTIST	PAGE
Anderson	Brown, Marianne	102
Boyle	Pointer, Judith	104
Calloway	Bates, Wayne	82
Calloway	O'Brian, Susan	84
Calloway	Shepard, Fred	86
Campbell	Watson, Larry	10
Casey	Reneau, Davie	72
Daviess	Dalton, Danny	88
Daviess	Dayman, Chris	90
Daviess	Driver, Steve	92
Daviess	Porter, Thomas	94
Daviess	Wethington, Cat	96
Fayette	Cerlan, Gayle	106
Fayette	Davis-Rosenbaum, Steve	108
Fayette	Glover, Don	110
Fayette	Goldstein, Susan	112
Fayette	Lipuma, Janice	114
Fayette	Molinaro, Joe	116
Fayette	Rice, Wyman	118
Fayette	Selter, Dan	120
Fayette	Sprengnether, Kate	122
Fayette	Spurlock, Liz	124
Fayette	Stofer, Jill Coldiron	126
Jefferson	Andre, Yerger	12
Jefferson	Austin, Lisa	14
Jefferson	Choo, Fong	16
Jefferson	Coakes, Michelle	18
Jefferson	Elswick, Amy,	20
Jefferson	Ferguson, Wayne	22
Jefferson	Frederick, Sarah	24
Jefferson	Leake, Peggy	26
Jefferson	Marsh, Ginny	28
Jefferson	Miner, Judy	30
Jefferson	Ross, Laura	32
Jefferson	Rounsavall, Mary	34
Jefferson	Rowe, Melvin	36
Jefferson	Temple, Byron	38
Kenton	England, Ana	40
Kenton	Kruer, Diane	44
Kenton	Oliver, Colette	42
Knott	Ware, Michael	52
Larue	Cochran, Jean	128
Madison	Cole, Teresa	54
Madison	Culbreth, Sarah	56
Madison	Enge, Jeff	56
Madison	Heffner, Gwen	58
Madison	Hyleck, Walter	60
Madison	Martin, John	62
Madison	Ripley, Trent	64
Madison	Wright, James	66
Mason	LeGris, Ann	46
McCracken	Roush, Sarah	98
Mercer	Carr, Cynthia	130
Mercer	Frasca, Michael	132
Mercer	Strecker, Chris	134
Mercer	Strecker, Zoe	136
Nelson	Zoeller, Michael	138
Owen	Seigel, Greg	48
Pulaski	McClorey, Meg	74
Rowan	Reitz, Tom	68
Warren	Rickman, Mitchell	76
Warren	Smith, Malcolm Mobutu	78

GALLERY	CITY	PHONE
A Niche in Time	Harrodsburg	859-733-9621
Appalachian Fireside Gallery	Berea	606-986-9013
Artifacts	Bowling Green	270-846-4004
Artique	Lexington	859-272-8802
Bebe's Artisan Market	Paducah	270-443-5848
Boone Tavern Gift Shop	Berea	606-986-9341
Bowery Gallery	Paducah	270-443-2582
Capital Gallery	Frankfort	502-223-2649
Chapman Gallery at Science Hill	Shelbyville	502-633-0204
Completely Kentucky	Frankfort	502-223-5240
Contemporary Artifacts Gallery	Berea	606-986-1096
Crooked Tree Gallery	Covington	606-261-6266
David Appalachian Crafts	David	606-886-2377
Dinner Bell Restaurant Gift Shop	Berea	606-986-2777
Edenside Gallery	Louisville	502-459-2787

galleries

Gallery 600	Paducah	270-442-1985
Gallery on the Square	Danville	606-936-1800
Harrodsburg General Store	Harrodsburg	606-734-6004
Harrodsburg Pottery and Crafts	Harrodsburg	606-734-9991
Images Friedman Gallery	Louisville	502-584-7954
Kentucky Art and Craft Foundation	Louisville	502-589-0102
Kentucky Haus	Newport	606-261-4287
Kentucky Horse Park	Lexington	859-233-4303
Loghouse Craft Gallery	Berea	859-986-4434
Louisville Visual Art Association	Louisville	502-581-1445
Main Cross Gallery	Lexington	859-258-9863
Marcum's Gallery	Louisville	502-426-7727
Marie Stewart Crafts Cabin	Hindman	606-785-9844
Moby Maple	Lexington	859-219-3022
Museum of the American Quilters Society	Paducah	270-898-7903
Owensboro Museum of Fine Art	Owensboro	270-685-3181
Piedmont Gallery	Augusta	606-756-2216
Pinecone Primitives	Somerset	606-677-1228
Promenade Gallery	Berea	606-986-1609
Raintree Gallery	Versailles	859-873-8822
Risch Gallery	Fort Thomas	606-441-3838
Scarborough Fare	Lexington	859-266-8704
Swanson Cralle Gallery	Louisville	502-452-2904
Tower Cerlan Gallery	Lexington	859-233-7284
True Kentucky	Glendale	270-369-7850
Upstairs Gallery	Berea	606-986-4434
Water Tower	Louisville	502-896-2146
Where in the World	Maysville	606-564-6815
White Gallery	Maysville	606-564-4887

galleries